SOUTHDOWN STYLE

Glyn Kraemer-Johnson

Capital Transport

Acknowledgements

My thanks go to all those who have helped me with the preparation of this book. The book would not have been possible without the photographs that have been supplied and, while the copyright holders have all been credited, I am grateful for their help. In particular I would like to thank the complete strangers that I have contacted via the internet, all of whom, without exception, have been only too happy to supply images.

My thanks go also to those who have supplied memorabilia, notably Howard Butler, Richard Maryan, Ian Richardson and the late Roger Knight. I am grateful to Andrew Dyer, late of Stagecoach South, for allowing me to use excerpts and illustrations from the Southdown in-house magazine. Finally, I would like to offer special thanks to Paul Gainsbury and Alan Lambert, not only for supplying material, but also for answering my endless questions over the past five years.

Glyn Kraemer-Johnson,
Westham, East Sussex, September 2015

First published 2015

ISBN 978-185414-396-9

Published by Capital Transport Publishing
www.capitaltransport.com

Printed by Parksons Graphics

Above For many years the Traffic Commissioners would not allow the operation of double-deckers to Beachy Head. As a compromise Southdown bought four Leyland Tiger three-axle single-deckers The first two, numbered 50/1 (AUF850/1) were classified TS6T and arrived in 1934. They were followed in 1935 by a further two based on the upgraded TS7T chassis and numbered 52/3 (BUF 552/3) All four had bodies by Short Bros seating 40 that were virtually to coach standards, and indeed they originally wore coach livery with script fleet names. All four had 500 added to their fleet numbers in 1937. Car 552 is seen on Eastbourne sea front, in full coach livery as originally worn by these vehicles. Note the destination blind showing 'Top of Beachy Head', as opposed to Eastbourne Corporation's open-top double-deckers, which had to terminate at the 'Foot of Beachy Head'. The steep climb to the summit would produce some amazing sound effects from 552's 8.6 litre engine. *(Southdown Enthusiasts' Club)*

Title page Nearing the end of its working life, but still showing the 'Southdown sparkle', 1434 (FCD 34) was one of the famous 1400 class of Harrington-bodied Leyland Tigers, which maintained the majority of Southdown's single-deck services throughout the thirties and forties, until replaced by the underfloor-engined Royal Tigers. Note that the side destination screens are still in use. *(W J Haynes/Southdown Enthusiasts' Club)*

All-Leyland PD1 315 (HCD 915) photographed in Basin Road, Chichester in May, 1963. It was working service 52A to Selsey, which originally paralleled Colonel Stephens' fascinating 'Hundred of Manhood and Selsey Tramway'. *(Southdown Enthusiasts' Club)*

Back cover Car 339 (JCD 39), a Leyland PD2/1 with Leyland bodywork, was one of a number of 'pre-1950' double-deckers to be fitted with three track route number boxes. It is seen on Worthing sea front in August 1962, with an open-top Guy Arab heading in the opposite direction. *(Southdown Enthusiasts' Club)*

Contents

Introduction	4
Setting the Style	8
Through Sussex and Beyond – Expansion and Consolidation	16
'Keeping the Wheels Turning'	30
'Enter the Titan'	31
The coaching side – Excursions, Tours and Express Services	34
On Stage – The stage-carriage fleet in the 1930s	46
Against all Odds – 1939-1945	50
Utilities on Parade	55
Renew and Repair – Post War Recovery	56
New Bodies for Old	62
A Bridge Too Weak	70
The Years of Plenty	72
'Unlucky 700'	77
'In Which They Served'	83
Best of the Breed	92
A new look – enter Mary and the Leopard	94
Decline and fall	104

Introduction

What makes a bus company special? Why is it that some operators are revered by enthusiasts and remembered with affection and respect by the travelling public whilst others went about their daily business, probably just as efficiently, without achieving such acclaim?

In the case of London Transport the reason is not too difficult to understand. It had a huge fleet, in excess of 7000 vehicles at its peak, mostly purpose-built and including the iconic RT and Routemaster. It also benefited from the glamour of operating in the capital, so much so that the red London bus has become virtually a national treasure. It has achieved celebrity status all over the world and many an old British bus that has never set tyres on the streets of London has been exported, painted red with London Transport on its sides and become a tourist attraction. Visitors to London buy cheap models of Routemasters to take home as souvenirs; one cannot imagine a bus in the livery of Grimsby or Stockport Corporations having the same appeal.

Outside London there was Midland Red, the country's second largest operator, which designed and built its own vehicles. Its designs were invariably innovative and advanced, setting the pattern for other manufacturers to follow and this naturally gave the company added interest and fascination.

Far from being innovative, Southdown Motor Services, if not third in the table then certainly in the top five, was traditional in the extreme. Apart from one very brief venture into Hovercraft operation and the introduction of a not very successful double deck coach, it followed the tried and tested. It remained faithful to the front-engined double-decker for as long as it could and ignored attempts by other operators to cram as many passengers as possible into its vehicles and to reduce vehicle weight at the expense of passenger comfort.

It has been said that there are two reasons for the popularity of a bus operator; both emanating from nostalgia. Firstly there was 'the bus we went to school on', which surely must apply to every operator in the country. Secondly, buses that bring back memories of happy holidays. With its operating area including the holiday resorts of Brighton, Eastbourne, Worthing and Littlehampton, this could well be true of Southdown, but then it could apply equally to East Kent, Southern Vectis, or Cumberland Motor Services, none of which has the same following as Southdown

The livery could have had something to do with it; the apple green, dark green and primrose was a classic amongst colour schemes, but not unique. The same colours were shared by Aldershot & District and, in pre-war days by a number of what were later to become Tilling-group companies.

Express services had a certain romance, the image of a dimly-lit motor coach speeding through the night from one end of the country to the other. But, whilst this may have been true of companies like Royal Blue and Standerwick, Southdown's express services ran mainly between London and the South Coast and were only of two or three hours' duration. The company was famous

As a result of the impressive performance of its utility Guy Arabs, Southdown made one of its fairly rare departures from Leyland and in 1948 took delivery of twelve Arab IIIs with Northern Counties bodywork. Divided between Brighton and Portsmouth, 509 (JCD 509) was one of Brighton's allocation and is seen at the Old Steine terminus of local service 109. An early Queen Mary waits behind. *(Southdown Enthusiasts' Club)*

for its coach holidays for which it offered an exceptionally high standard of quality and comfort. However, while the internal specification was luxurious the coaches themselves were mostly 'off the peg' with external mouldings and embellishments to give them individuality and Southdown's style.

Style. Perhaps that's the word for which we are looking. One dictionary gives the definition of 'style' as 'a combination of distinctive features'. This was certainly true of Southdown. Quality, luxury, elegance, reliability, service and impeccable presentation, Southdown had them all. Mention has already been made of its livery which, whilst not unique was certainly distinctive and blended in so well with the Sussex countryside through which its buses passed. Moreover it was immaculately maintained. Dents and scratches were dealt with promptly and the paintwork itself was maintained to such a high standard that it earned the name of 'the Southdown Sparkle'. Internally, both on coaches and stage carriage vehicles a high standard of comfort was specified with unusually comfortable seats well spaced to give plenty of legroom. One independent operator who purchased some former Southdown double-deckers was quoted as saying: "I can't believe that buses of this standard were used on daily bus services". For very many years the interior colour scheme was mainly of various shades of browns and cream. Some said it was drab but in the writer's opinion it was conservative, subdued and spoke of quality.

Certainly in the Brighton area the comparison was marked. On one hand were Brighton Corporation's faded art-deco, Brighton, Hove & District's practical but utilitarian Tilling Group interior and then Southdown's hint of luxury. Southdown's buses had heaters, something unknown on the vehicles of the other two operators until 1959! Its touring coaches were in a class of their own, with 2+1 seating for those employed on extended tours, or 'Coach Cruises' as they were known and were regular winners at the British Coach Rally. It has been related many times that for an hotelier to have a Southdown coach parked outside was a recommendation for his establishment. On at least one occasion a broken down tour coach was towed back to Brighton under cover of darkness, lest it should create a bad image.

Southdown adopted a style of its own from very early days, thanks largely to what could have been called a number of idiosyncrasies. Vehicles were always referred to as 'cars', never as buses or coaches, which apparently stemmed from Alfred Douglas Mackenzie's intense dislike of the term 'motor-bus'. The buses were equipped with a multitude of destination blinds; in the early days three on each side as well as front and rear. For many years vehicles were fitted with metal sun-visors above the windscreen, which gave them a distinctive if rather scowling appearance. With the introduction of the under-floor engined chassis Southdown purchased a batch of Leyland Royal Tiger coaches with Duple Ambassador bodies, the mouldings and embellishments on which it adopted as standard on most of the Company's coaches until the early 1960s, giving them an instantly recognisable and distinctive appearance. Similarly the first underfloor-engined saloons, again Royal Tigers but with East Lancs bodywork, featured a vee-shaped moulding below the windscreen, which again was perpetuated on most of the Company's single-deckers.

When its neighbouring operators were ordering high-capacity double-deckers, Southdown stuck rigidly to its 59 seats and even when the maximum length was increased to 30 feet the capacity went up only to 69. These buses were of course what were to become known as the 'Queen Marys' and which, for some reason which has never been quite clear to the writer, became almost as iconic as the Routemaster. After all it was little more than a standard forward-entrance double-decker with what to me, at least, was a rather ugly and ungainly full front, although I have no doubt that my comments will be met with howls of protest from its many fans!

Those who have read the companion volume 'Midland Red Style' will have noted the wealth of brightly-coloured publicity material produced by that company. Not so Southdown. Most of its leaflets and brochures were produced in monotone green whilst its main timetable carried the same picture on its cover for very many years. The information was provided without unnecessary frills and presumably expense! We have tried to find some of the more colourful examples for inclusion in this book.

Southdown was a fascinating company with many idiosyncrasies but with a reputation for high standards of comfort and service and, for whatever reason, it is still held in high regard by enthusiasts and the people who travelled on its 'cars', whether it was an open-top bus ride to Beachy Head, a luxury coach holiday to Switzerland or simply the daily journey to and from work or school. Hopefully the pages that follow will go some way to explain the reason for its popularity and to show in words and pictures just what was 'Southdown Style'.

WALTER FLEXMAN FRENCH

The son of an Essex dairy farmer, Walter Flexman-French studied at the Imperial College of Science & Technology at South Kensington, after which he worked in general engineering for some years before setting up his own bicycle manufacturing business in Balham, south London. However, he had an interest in and a desire to improve the internal combustion engine and this led to him becoming the first person to operate a petrol-engined stage carriage vehicle in London, which he ran on a route from Putney to Piccadilly Circus. The venture was not entirely successful as the all-too frequent stops caused problems with the gear boxes. French therefore moved on to a quieter route running from Clapham Junction to Streatham.

He was involved in motor-bus operation in a number of places including Guildford, Margate and Maidstone. In 1910 he purchased an operation running a service between Maidstone and Chatham which he named the 'Maidstone, Chatham, Gravesend and District Motor Omnibus Service'. The following year it was renamed 'The Maidstone & District Motor Services Ltd' and French appointed his son, George as Managing Director of the new company.

When he gave up the manufacture of bicycles he set up a garage in Balham under the name of French's Garage and Motor Works Ltd and then, in 1904 he moved to Worthing as manager of the Sussex Motor Road Car Co Ltd. He managed the company for two years before placing it in the hands of Mackenzie and Canon and returning to London. He then set up a haulage company, the London & South Coast Haulage Co Ltd. The venture did not prove as profitable as had been expected and so French turned his attention to what he knew best; the motor-bus. He began a service from Brighton to Hurstpierpoint and followed this by purchasing a company with the most unlikely name of 'Jolly Jumbo's'!

In 1915 the London & South Coast Haulage Co became one of the three major constituent companies of Southdown Motor Services Ltd.

Worthing Motor Services DL 705 with 'Sussex Tourist Coaches' fleet name. It was a Daimler CC/Hora 30-seat body new in 4/14. The chassis was requisitioned after just five months and the body was re-used by Southdown at a later date. The main interest however is not so much in the bus as the people. To the left of the coach, with beard and characteristic seaman-style hat, is Alfred Douglas Mackenzie whilst, second from the left in the main group is Alfred Cannon. *(Southdown Chronicle/Stagecoach South)*

ALFRED DOUGLAS MACKENZIE

Mackenzie was of Scottish stock although born in Kensington and was an early transport enthusiast and 'spotter', having collected railway locomotive numbers as a schoolboy. For this he devised a methodical classification system to make the task easier, a hint of the superlative ticketing and numbering systems that he was to introduce to Southdown in later life, and which led him to register his vehicles in Brighton, West Sussex, the Isle of Wight and even County Armagh in Northern Ireland in order to procure the 'matching' numbers he wanted. He was apprenticed to a firm of marine engineers in Sunderland and undertook several voyages in the course of his training, which possibly accounted for the neatly trimmed beard and seaman's-style peaked cap for which he was well known.

Following his apprenticeship he was appointed as a qualified steam engineer by the National Traction Engine Owners' Association, which set him the task of assessing the country roads and bridges for strength and suitability for use by traction engines. This task took him from the Lake District to Cornwall and

planted in his mind the idea that one day it would be possible to operate long-distance tours, taking the ordinary man-in-the-street to some of the most beautiful places in England; places which most would never have seen. Thus was sown the seed that blossomed into the Coach Cruises for which Southdown was to become renowned.

After a spell managing a fleet of steam-powered vehicles near Oxford, Mackenzie foresaw that the future of the transport industry lay with the internal combustion engine and thus set about increasing his experience and knowledge of this form of propulsion. Having done so he set himself up as an engineering consultant in London and it was in this capacity that he first had contact with the Isle of Wight Express Motor Syndicate, which was in the hands of one Frank Bartlett, a man who was to play an important part in the formation of Southdown Motor Services. It was also at this time that Mackenzie designed his famous 'slipper-style' charabanc with its rows of seats ascending towards the rear, which in this instance was supplied to the Clacton-on-Sea Motor Omnibus Company. He was called in when the Isle of

Wight Express Motor Syndicate went into receivership and then, in April 1907 he was appointed as full-time General Manager of the Sussex Motor Road Car Co. Ltd. Following the voluntary liquidation of the SMRCC, he formed Worthing Motor Services, a direct constituent of Southdown. A few months before the formation of Southdown, however, Mackenzie and Alfred Cannon were responsible for the formation of another company, Wilts & Dorset Motor Services Ltd which, hardly surprisingly, was run on very similar lines to Southdown.

ALFRED EDWARD CANNON

Writing his obituary in the Southdown house magazine 'Tweenus' in 1952, the then Chairman, R P Beddow wrote of Alfred Cannon 'The finest memorial which Mr Cannon could have is the Southdown undertaking, and it is indeed his memorial. The Southdown traditions, of which we are justly proud, were built up in the main under Mr Cannon's inspiration and leadership. We cannot better honour the memory of the man who was a friend to so many of us, than by doing our best to cherish and foster these traditions. By so doing, we shall keep his memory green.'

Not a great deal appears to have been recorded about the early life of Alfred Edward Cannon, other than that he was born in Oxfordshire in 1883 and served his engineering apprenticeship with the Great Western Railway at Wolverhampton. He later worked for the Power Omnibus Company in London before joining Mackenzie at Worthing in 1907 in an attempt to save the fortunes of the Sussex Motor Road Car Co. In this they did not succeed but managed to salvage sufficient vehicles to form Worthing Motor Services. Together with Mackenzie he went on to form Wilts & Dorset Motor Services Ltd in January 1915 and later in the same year brought about the birth of Southdown Motor Services. This was, of course, the time of the Great War and almost immediately Cannon was called on to serve his country by joining the Railway Operations Division of the Royal Engineers. Following his return to Brighton in 1919 the company grew rapidly from a fleet of around 100 to 600 by 1935.

In his spare time he played tennis, badminton and golf and sailed a Dutch sailing barge, the *Santa Maria,* from Bosham. His real hobby, however, was Southdown Motor Services. Cannon was the man responsible for the company's high standards of maintenance and cleanliness that led to the epithet 'the Southdown Sparkle'.

Alfred Edward Cannon in later life.
(Southdown Chronicle/Stagecoach South)

FRANK BARTLETT

Bartlett was born at Ryde in the Isle of Wight in 1860, starting work as a telegraph boy and junior clerk at the age of 12. His introduction to the transport industry came five years later when he joined the Ryde Pier Company as booking clerk for the Isle of Wight Joint Railway Companies at Ryde Esplanade and Pier Head stations. He then moved to Portsmouth taking up a similar position at Fratton and Southsea stations. After a spell in Canada he returned to his native island and set up his own business arranging steamship excursions and undertaking emigration work from his Portsmouth office.

In 1905 he contacted the Isle of Wight Express Motor Syndicate with a suggestion that there was an opportunity for running motor bus services and excursions in Portsmouth. Although the suggestion was not taken up it was through this that Bartlett met Mackenzie and became involved in the Sussex Motor Road Car and Worthing Motor Services. On its formation he joined Southdown and was largely responsible for establishing the Portsmouth depot.

SIDNEY GARCKE

Chairman of Southdown from 1926 to 1946, Sidney Garcke was born in London in January, 1885. He studied at London University after which he joined the British Electric Traction Company, a concern started by his father. He was keenly interested in the development of the motor bus and helped with experiments with this form of transport being carried out in Birmingham. The terrain proved too hilly, however, and in 1908 he used some of the buses used in Birmingham to start a service in Deal on the Kent Coast, laying the foundations for the East Kent Road Car Co of which he was to be Chairman for 29 years. He established bus operations in many parts of the country and invested in a number of existing companies, the first being the Aldershot & District Traction Co.

During the 1914-18 war he served as officer commanding the Berkshire R.A.S.C., M.T., with the rank of major. He resigned his position as managing director of the B.A.T. at the end of 1918 in order to devote more personal attention to the associated companies, but retained his seat on the board and was appointed as chairman in April 1923. He became a director of the parent B.E.T. in 1928, and held that office until his death. Following the Railway-Road Transport Act of 1928 he was very much involved with the co-ordination of road and rail services. In 1943 he joined the boards of Dennis Bros, and the Eastwood Brick Company but thereafter began to relinquish his executive positions. In 1946 he resigned as Chairman of Aldershot & District, East Kent, Maidstone & District and Southdown. He died in October 1948.

Setting the Style

Southdown Motor Services Ltd was formed in June 1915 from three major constituent companies, Worthing Motor Services, The London & South Coast Haulage Co, and the country services of the Brighton, Hove & Preston United Omnibus Company Ltd. The fact that Southdown's style existed from the very beginning was due in no small part to its four main founders, Walter Flexman French, Alfred Douglas Mackenzie, Alfred Edward Cannon and Frank Bartlett.

Worthing Motor Services was the largest contributor to the newly-formed company in terms of vehicles, employees and, of course the basis of what was to become the Southdown livery. Motorbus services in Worthing had started in 1904 with the formation of the Sussex Motor Road Car Co Ltd, which was founded under the auspices of Walter Flexman French. His is a name that crops up regularly throughout the Southdown story.

In July 1904 two Clarkson steam buses were purchased and put to work on a service between Worthing and Pulborough via Findon, Washington and Storrington, which later had the distinction of becoming Southdown service 1. Travelling on the service was quite an adventure as passengers could never be sure whether or not they would complete the journey due to breakdowns, most of which were caused by the furring-up of the boilers brought about by the hard, chalky water of the area. Attempts were made to cure the problem by installing underground tanks beneath the White Horse Hotel, Storrington for the collection of rainwater. Unfortunately it was a year of drought and after six months the steam buses were withdrawn and sold, being replaced by Milnes-Daimler petrol-engined single-deckers. The service proved popular, offering many passengers their first opportunity to ride in a 'horseless carriage' and higher fares were charged for the front seats. Further services were introduced between Worthing, Littlehampton and Arundel and from Pulborough to Hove via Steyning, but the real objective was Brighton.

In November 1904 the Worthing Motor Omnibus Company was formed, initially to introduce a town service in competition with the local horse bus operator but which later gained a licence to operate a route from Worthing to Palmeira Square in Hove, the reason for the turning point being that Brighton Council would not give permission for the service to continue into their Borough. The following year the Worthing Motor Omnibus Company and the Sussex Motor Road Car Company joined forces running under the latter's fleet name. Brighton Council finally agreed that the service could run into the Borough but would not consent to the Aquarium being used as a terminus, insisting that the buses should continue via St James's Street to Kemp Town. Fearful of having its territory invaded the Brighton Hove and Preston United Omnibus Co applied for and was granted a licence to operate a similar service between Brighton and Worthing.

The Brighton Hove & Preston United Omnibus Co Ltd was the oldest of the three companies which would form Southdown Motor Services, having been established in 1884 by the amalgamation of a number of Brighton's horse bus operators. The company's stables and garage were in Conway Street, Hove, on the site now occupied by the Head Offices of the Brighton & Hove Bus and Coach Co Ltd.

In the same year the Brighton District Tramway Company opened a 3ft 6in gauge tramway running steam-hauled double-deck trams from Shoreham via the coast road to Portslade where it turned inland, proceeding via New Church Road to the top of Westbourne Villas. This terminus was again made necessary by Brighton Council's refusal to allow the tramway to continue further eastward. In consequence agreement was reached for a connecting horse bus service to run via Church Road and Western Road to Castle Square in the centre of the town. In 1889 the British Electric Traction Company acquired an interest in the tramway with a view to its electrification, but local opposition was so strong that this never happened and the line eventually closed in 1912.

Having built up a network of services in its 'home towns' of Brighton and Hove, the BH&PU began to look further afield, applying for licences to operate to Lewes, Newhaven and Hurstpierpoint although it is not clear if these routes were ever operated as Brighton Corporation objected to BH&PU buses running over roads that were served by its trams. What was operated of course was the Worthing service, which ran in competition with the Sussex Motor Road Car Co.

Unfortunately passenger loadings were insufficient to support both operators and the SMRC soon found it was running at a loss. Experiments were made with timings so that the Road Cart buses ran in front of instead of behind the BHPU vehicles and a request was made to Brighton Council for the unremunerative section between Kemp Town and the Aquarium to be withdrawn, but this was refused.

By this time Walter Flexman French had returned to London and it was decided that someone with a good experience of bus operation should be brought in to try and save the Road Car Company. The chosen person was one Alfred Douglas Mackenzie who was appointed as General Manager and who brought with him Mr Alfred Cannon who had been with the Pioneer Motor Omnibus Company in London, as its Chief Engineer. Mackenzie's recipe to put the Company back on its feet was expansion. He purchased three Thornycroft single-deckers with bodies to what was to become his famous 'slipper' design, in essence charabancs with rows of seats ascending towards the rear. They had Isle of Wight registrations DL 208/9/61 and were put to work on the Brighton service. He also introduced a new service between Bognor and Portsmouth, the idea being that eventually it would be extended to Littlehampton, thus providing a through service between Brighton and Portsmouth. Loadings on the Portsmouth section were poor, however and due to this and the loss-making Brighton service, in the winter of 1908/9, the Company found itself unable to pay the rent on its Portsmouth premises and the Portsmouth-based vehicles were rapidly transferred to Worthing to prevent their seizure. In September 1908 the company went into voluntary liquidation.

Milnes Daimler BP 311, one of the short-lived Worthing Motor Omnibus Company vehicles. This was the operator that launched the Worthing to Hove service but subsequently joined forces with the Sussex Motor Road Car Co. *(Glyn Kraemer-Johnson Collection)*

Worthing Motor Services single-decker DL 701, another example, of Mackenzie's 'slipper' design of charabanc body with rows of seats rising towards the rear. A disadvantage of the original design was that, with a full load, much of the weight was high and behind the rear wheels; not the best recipe for stability! *(Glyn Kraemer-Johnson Collection)*

Mackenzie, however, was not a man to admit defeat easily and he managed to retain sufficient vehicles to operate the Storrington service through the winter of that year and, in March 1909, formed a new company, Worthing Motor Services Ltd, which took over the SMRC premises in Worthing. Mackenzie wasted no time in applying for a licence to operate to Brighton, but regulations had been tightened and neither Hove nor Brighton Corporations would allow Worthing Motor Services to pick up passengers east of Portslade, while Worthing Corporation imposed similar restrictions on Brighton, Hove and Preston United buses entering the town. However, in 1912 the situation was resolved when agreement was reached between the two companies whereby WMS would withdraw from the route in exchange for 5% of United's revenue.

Mackenzie introduced excursions to race meetings and in 1913 fulfilled a long-held ambition by introducing extended tours to the West Country, Wales and the Lake District. These were operated under the fleet name of 'Sussex Tourist Coaches'.

Re-enter Walter Flexman French. Following his return to London, French had set up a haulage business under the name of the London & South Coast Haulage Co Ltd, which was not proving as financially viable as had been expected. French therefore turned his attention to what he knew best - the motorbus. He applied for and was granted a licence to operate a service from Brighton to Hurstpierpoint, which was later extended to Burgess Hill. He then purchased a family concern running under the almost surreal name of 'Jolly Jumbo's'.

August 1914 saw the outbreak of the First World War and it was not long before bus operators began to face severe difficulties. The Military requisitioned the best chassis, leaving the unwanted bodies behind. With their fleets thus depleted the operators found themselves endeavouring to cope with an increase in passengers. It therefore became a case of unity in adversity with the three companies helping each other out where they could. The result was the realisation that in the circumstances co-operation was preferable to competition and it was therefore agreed that the three operators should form themselves into one single company. Thus in April 1915 Worthing Motor Services, the London and South Coast Haulage Co and the country services and excursions of the Brighton Hove & Preston United Omnibus Co Ltd were amalgamated to form a new company known as South Coast Motor

From the BH&PU came a number of Milnes Daimler coaches with bodies by either Dodson or BH&PU itself, which resembled the Worthing Motor Services design. The body pictured here was built by Dodson and was originally fitted to BH&PU CD 509. In 1916 it was transferred to Southdown 92 (IB 805), a Scout acquired from sister company Wilts & Dorset. *(Glyn Kraemer-Johnson Collection)*

A timetable issued under the short-lived 'South Coast Motor Services' title. The company was known by that name for a mere two months from April to June 1915, this timetable being issued in May of that year. *(Michael Rooum Collection)*

Three months later, in July 1915, a new timetable was issued, this time with the new name of 'Southdown Motor Services' on the cover. *(Author's Collection)*

The charabanc reigned supreme throughout the nineteen-twenties. No.423 (UF 2023) was a 1927 Tilling Stevens B9B with Harrington 29-seat charabanc body and was presumably on a private hire duty when this photograph was taken with a full load of passengers posing for the camera. The vehicle had a quite interesting history, being fitted with a fixed back in 1930 before being rebodied with a new Harrington 30-seat coach body in 1934. Sold to Wilts & Dorset in 1939, it was commandeered by Southern Command in 1940 and ended its days working for the Secretary of State at the Home Office. *(Southdown Enthusiasts' Club/Alan Lambert)*

The original fleet name style was simplified until the style shown here was reached. In this form the script fleet name was applied to coaches and to some buses until the absorption of Southdown into the National Bus Company. Even after that an excuse was found for it to be applied to a handful of coaches! *(Southdown Enthusiasts' Club)*

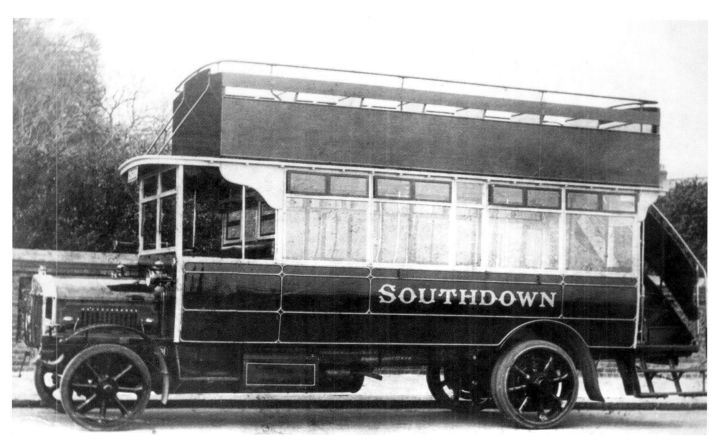

Whilst not as elegant as the Mackenzie script fleet name used for coaches, that applied to stage carriage vehicles was distinctive and ornate with embellishments on every letter. The bus is probably a Tilling-Stevens TS3A with a Tilling 51-seat body. *(Southdown Enthusiasts' Club)*

Services Ltd. However, there was a last minute change of heart and on 2 June 1915 it was registered as Southdown Motor Services Ltd with a capital of £51,250. This figure gradually increased until by 1964 it stood at £3,600,000. The Company was launched with the 'Three Wise Men' at the helm. Walter Flexman French was appointed chairman, with Alfred Cannon as Managing Director and Alfred Douglas Mackenzie as Traffic Manager.

In January 1915 McKenzie and Cannon had registered the Wilts & Dorset company and there was for many years a similarity and close relationship between the two companies, which even went as far as Wilts & Dorset vehicles being ordered by Southdown. In fact it could have been said that Wilts & Dorset was in reality a 'red Southdown'.

The Southdown livery of apple green, dark green and primrose was clearly adapted from that of Worthing Motor Services and, although simplified over the years the basic colour scheme remained the same until the advent of the National Bus Company. Stage carriage vehicles carried the name 'SOUTHDOWN' in large, ornate block capitals in gold with black shading to the left and below. It was not practical to apply fleet names to the sides of charabancs, only the rear, so it was not until 1922, when the centre

gangway had become the norm that the famous script fleet name, began to appear on the sides of all coaches, together with a number of single-deck buses and a few double-deckers, in particular the Guy open-toppers, again continuing in use until replaced by the standard NBC-style of fleet name. Even after that it appeared on a few selected vehicles.

From the start Southdown found itself with a motley collection of vehicles, a situation not helped by expansion and the purchase of smaller operators and the vehicles. The constituent companies contributed some thirty-four vehicles. Fifteen came from Worthing Motor Services, mainly of Milnes Daimler and Daimler manufacture but including a Leyland X, a Straker Squire and a couple of Tilling-Stevens TS3s. The BH&PU contributed eleven coaches on Milnes Daimler, Daimler and Straker-Squire chassis, with closed bodies of the 'slipper' design, similar to those of Worthing Motor Services. Also from the Brighton company came fourteen spare bodies from chassis commandeered by the Army. Also from BH&PU came 19 horses and a number of horse-drawn carriages and charabancs, some of which were operated by Southdown throughout the summer of 1916. A further five spare bodies came from the London & South Coast Haulage Co together with eight complete vehicles of Daimler, Leyland and Straker Squire manufacture plus four Durham Churchill chassis with Harrington charabanc bodies, the beginning of a very long association between Southdown and the Hove coachbuilder.

As well as vehicles a number of properties were also transferred to the new company. These included the former Worthing Motor Services Ivy Arch garage at Broadwater Road, Worthing, the garage at Storrington, premises at Marine Parade, Worthing, including what was known as 'Mackenzie's Counting House', accommodation at Newhaven and Seaford and the Royal Mews, Steine Street, Brighton. The Brighton, Hove & Preston United Company contributed its Steyne Garage in Worthing, land between Park Street and Freshfield Road in Brighton (later to become the Brighton coach garage), offices at 6 Pavilion Buildings, Brighton, which for a time served as the new company's head office, and the stables and workshops in Upper St James's Street. From the London & South Coast Haulage Company came its premises in Middle Street, Brighton.

And so, with vehicles, property and a management team, the scene was set and the foundations laid for what was to become one of the UK's largest and most respected bus and coach operators.

The original fleet name (Left) continued in use until after the Second World War, when it was simplified by the removal of some of the embellishments on the letters (Below left)

In the 1970s a more modern and much simplified, though not necessarily more attractive, style was introduced using plain block letters. A similar style was introduced for the Southdown-BH&D fleet.

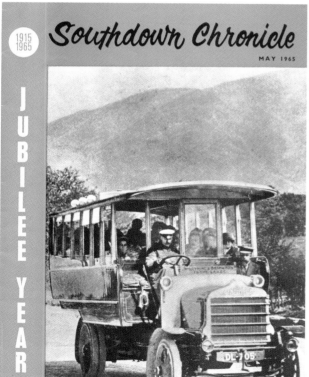

1915 1965

Southdown Chronicle

MAY 1965

JUBILEE YEAR

During World War 1 it was a case not only of buying what was available, but also of choosing makes that were not likely to be requisitioned by the Military, and this led to a number of unusual makes being taken into the fleet. One such was number 22 (CD 3322), a rare McCurd bought new in 1915, which, in spite of its Scottish-sounding name, was actually built in London. It was fitted with a Brighton Hove & Preston bus body, one of the 'spare' bodies acquired from that company. Longer than usual, it seated 36, an unusually high number for the time. The long rear overhang is clearly visible in this picture. *(Alan Lambert)*

To mark its Golden Jubilee in 1965 Southdown chose to publish this picture of Worthing Motor Services Milnes Daimler DL 705 on the cover of its house magazine, 'The Southdown Chronicle'. *(The Southdown Chronicle/Stagecoach South)*

Through Sussex and Beyond – Expansion and Consolidation

The first new vehicles taken into stock in 1915 did little to aid stand-ardisation. This was wartime, remember, and it was very much a case of 'take what you can get'. Thus although there were some well-known makes such as Tilling-Stevens and Straker-Squire, there were also some less familiar types including McCurd, Caledon and Romar. While these were new chassis, many of the bodies were those taken from vehicles requisitioned by the Army. Once estab-lished, however it began to standardise mainly on Tilling-Stevens and Leyland, the latter company of course becoming Southdown's major supplier for the next 60 years.

A number of horse-drawn charabancs had been inherited from the Brighton, Hove & Preston company and during the summer of 1915 these were used to operate excursions from Brighton to such places as Devil's Dyke. In 1916, however, when more stringent petrol rationing came into force, these vehicles came into their own. The Great War also saw a number of buses converted to run on town gas. Unlike the trailers used in the Second World War, the gas was carried in ungainly bags fitted to the roofs. They were moderately successful, managing to cover reasonable distances between 'refills', but towards the end of the war, gas became subject to the same restrictions as petrol, thus taking away the advantages and the Company abandoned the idea.

The first operators to be acquired were Mantell's horse-brake business in Brighton, bought purely for its licences, and the busi-ness of A Davis of Bognor, which brought with it three Commer charabancs, but again the main attraction was the licences, which included a service from Bognor to Chichester and Portsmouth. The licence was not immediately used but was eventually to form part of Southdown's premier service 31 between Brighton and Southsea. Mr Davis himself was made Manager at Bognor.

A 1962 view of the imposing Bognor Bus Station opened in 1934, its fine Art Deco frontage seeming to have much in common with contemporary Odeon cinemas. Even the style of lettering used for the Southdown name has been changed to blend in with the overall appearance. *(Southdown Enthusiasts' Club)*

For many years two Eastern Coachworks-bodied Leyland PS1s could be found at Bognor serving as Left Luggage Offices. Originally numbered 1229 (GUF 729) and 1249 (HCD 449), they were renumbered as 691 and 689 on demotion to bus work in 1956/7 and had a 'D' prefix added on conversion to Left Luggage offices. This rear nearside view of D689 (HCD 449) shows off the pleasing lines of the ECW 'Express' single-deck body and also the rather strange half-drop windows fitted to these coaches. Even when in use as a Left Luggage office it still looked immaculate, the roof boards adding a nice touch. *(Cliff Essex)*

A garage was included in the purchase of the Davies business that was used by Southdown for a while until the Portsmouth service was withdrawn in 1916. In 1919 a building situated on the corner of Richmond and Station Roads was purchased, which was constructed largely of corrugated iron. Following a disastrous fire in 1923 it was rebuilt using bricks. 1934 saw the opening of a brand new bus station in High Street, Bognor, the façade of which was a fine example of Art Deco architecture. In 1957 the Richmond Road garage was exchanged for a site behind the bus station and in this form the combined bus station and garage served the town until closed by the National Bus Company in 1980.

During the war, Alfred Cannon served with the Royal Engineers and Mackenzie acted as both General Manager and Traffic Manager until his return in 1919 when they resumed their respective positions. There is little doubt that the early success of Southdown was due in no small part to the men at the top. Mackenzie had fixed ideas on timetables and scheduling, believing that if an hourly service would not pull in the punters, a half-hourly one probably would (present day managers take note!). This had been tried and tested with Wilts & Dorset where daily services running on a half-hourly frequency were seeing increasing traffic while neighbouring Southern National, operating services once or twice a week on market days was losing passengers to the increasingly popular motor car, traffic which it would be difficult if not impossible to regain. Thus was laid down the foundation of Southdown's schedules, which were to become something of a legend, renowned for

its connecting services. A perfect example of this was the Heath-field Pool whereby services from Brighton, Eastbourne, Hastings, Hawkhurst and Tunbridge Wells all connected at Heathfield, effectively doubling the frequency of services between these points. But more of that later.

Following the end of the First World War in 1918 Southdown found traffic increasing considerably. Not only did the holiday and excursion trade return but people began to realise the benefits of living in the beautiful countryside and temperate climate of Sussex. Consequently there was much development, particularly along the coastal strip where settlements sprang up that were politely called 'bungalow towns'. These were in reality no more than shanty towns, many of the dwellings being converted railway carriages. Not aesthetically pleasing but bread and butter to Cannon and Mackenzie.

With Southdown's operating area stretching along the South Coast, eventually extending from Portsmouth in the west to Eastbourne in the east, a distance of some 60 miles, it soon became apparent that it was not possible to manage the company efficiently from one central point and so five separate areas were created based on Portsmouth, Bognor, Chichester, Worthing, Brighton and Eastbourne. Each area had a central garage and workshops capable of carrying out routine maintenance and repairs and an Area Manager was placed in charge of each. These were no cosy office-bound positions, the Managers being expected to rule firmly and ensure that instructions were carried out to the letter. If this meant supervising the departure of vehicles from an isolated country garage at 4.30 am on a cold, winter morning, then so be it. Again, it was this kind of discipline that made Southdown the revered and respected company it was to become. To recount the development that took place during the 1920s, it is probably practical to look at each of the five areas in turn.

Even as early as the autumn of 1915 garage accommodation was becoming a problem, especially in the Brighton area. Work was therefore started on building a garage and workshops on the land between Park Street and Freshfield Road that had been inherited from the BH&PU Company. Opened in 1916 it not only provided covered accommodation for most of the Brighton-based fleet, but also maintenance and repair facilities sufficient for it to become the company's Central Works in which capacity it continued until 1928 when new and much larger premises were built at Portslade. During this time the complex was expanded both in Park Street and by the purchase of more property in Freshfield Road itself. One such purchase made in 1938 was of 29 Freshfield Road, which had once been All Souls' Vicarage. The garage built on the site not unnaturally became known as 'The Vicarage' and eventually became home to the Brighton Area engineer. The long narrow garage that ran between Park Street and Freshfield Road was in later days used mainly for the storage of touring coaches during the winter months.

Office accommodation too was at a premium. Much as Cannon and particularly Mackenzie preferred to work in Worthing, Southdown's Head Office had been situated in Brighton from the outset. Initially the registered offices were at Middle Street in the premises inherited from the London & South Coast Haulage Co and which had originally been the property of 'Jolly Jumbo'. Some adminis-trative work was also undertaken at the former Brighton Hove & Preston United's premises at 6 Pavilion Buildings. However, one Stuart Smith, a livery stable owner, had allowed his premises at Royal Mews, Steine Street to be used by Worthing Motor Services and subsequently by Southdown. Smith lived in Steine Street and eventually his house was acquired by Southdown. Thus the company's Head Office was established at 5 Steine Street, Brighton, the address that was to appear on the side of every vehicle for almost fifty years.

During the ensuing years most of the properties on the west side of Manchester Street, which backed on to the Steine Street buildings were also acquired and eventually housed not only the Head Offices but also most of the Brighton Area offices.

The area to the north of the offices became Southdown's Brighton Coach Station and illustrated the company's apparent liking for bus and coach stations with difficult access. The coach station was roughly L-shaped and had capacity for around half a dozen coaches. The entrance was in Manchester Street, a narrow street running parallel to Steine Street, which in turn was accessed from St James's Street, a busy, narrow thoroughfare, which at that time carried two-way traffic including trolleybuses. On summer Saturdays in the fifties coaches waiting to enter the coach station would block Manchester Street and stretch back into St James's Street causing chaos!

With routes stretching from Brighton along the coast to the extremities of the Southdown area, eastwards to Eastbourne and to the west the long trek to Portsmouth, the company set about expanding its inland services and established routes fanning out from Brighton to Lewes, Uckfield, Haywards Heath, Chelwood Gate, Horsham and Petworth. In 1920 it introduced the first

'Mackenzie's Counting House' as it was known, otherwise number 23 Marine Parade, Worthing. Originally in the ownership of Worthing Motor Services, for many years the building housed Douglas Mackenzie's Traffic Department and it was from here that not only the affairs of Southdown were managed, but also those of Wilts & Dorset. Standing before it is Southdown 90 (CD 5590), a Tilling Stevens TS3 with Harrington 32-seat charabanc body. The vehicle was new in 1920 and later received an open-top double-deck body. The building survived in Southdown ownership until the Company's take-over by Stagecoach. (Alan Lambert Collection)

Head Office; 5 Steine Street, Brighton, the address that appeared on the side of every vehicle. In the centre is the Coach Station exit and to its right, the entrance to the Booking Office. *(Southdown Enthusiasts' Club)*

of what were to become many services operated jointly with neighbouring Maidstone & District Motor Services Ltd, this being the 18 to Heathfield and Hawkhurst, just across the Kent border.

Expanding services together with the thriving workshops at Freshfield Road soon resulted in the need for more accommodation in the Brighton area and in 1924 land was purchased at the lower end of Edward Street, close to the famous Royal Pavilion. A garage was built solely for the accommodation of vehicles, although a couple of inspection pits were added later. With its entrance in Edward Street and an exit leading onto Grand Parade it was ideally situated for vehicles terminating near the Palace Pier, or later in Pool Valley to return to the garage for refuelling or minor maintenance between journeys.

In 1928 the workshops at Freshfield Road were transferred to a new Central Works built in Victoria Road, Portslade, fully described later in this volume. Since the Company's formation, the Brighton terminus for stage-carriage services had been adjacent to the Aquarium in Madeira Drive. Although a waiting room

was provided it was probably not the most welcoming of places when there was a force 10 blowing off the sea! A bus station was eventually established in 1929 when Brighton Corporation gave permission for Southdown to use Pool Valley, a triangular site bordered to the north by Royal York Buildings, newly acquired by the Corporation for office accommodation and to the east by the Albion Hotel. The western side had been the site of 'Brill's Baths' but this had been demolished and replaced by the Savoy Cinema, which opened in January 1930 and against whose long, blank wall Southdown buses would lay over between duties. The narrow end of the triangle opened on to the sea front and acted like a funnel, the wind blowing in from the sea and swirling around inside the 'Valley' before managing to escape.

It was another example of Southdown's apparent penchant for bus stations and garages with difficult access, buses having to swing out into the busy traffic of Old Steine before turning into the narrow entrance to Pool Valley. However, it served Southdown well into the NBC era and was probably the most photographed location in the Southdown area.

THE SOUTHDOWN CHRONICLE

TWEENUS

An interior view of Edward Street Garage in the early nineteen-sixties and showing a fascinating collection of vehicles including a PD2/1. PD2/12, Guy Arab IV and several PD3s. On the right can be seen an East Lancs-bodied Royal Tiger and, next to it an all-Leyland Royal Tiger coach demoted to bus duties. In the left foreground are a Ford Transit service van and a Leyland TD towing vehicle, originally a bus. *(Southdown Enthusiasts' Club)*

This passengers' eye view of rush hour in Pool Valley was featured on the cover of the August 1959 issue of the 'Southdown Chronicle'. *(Southdown Chronicle/Stagecoach South)*

East Lancs-bodied PD2/12 800 (RUF 200) arrives in Pool Valley at the end of its long journey from Gravesend on service 122, a route operated jointly with Maidstone & District. The view illustrates just how narrow was the entrance road. It became more difficult to negotiate as the length of buses increased and eventually the pavement on the left-hand side was removed to improve access and pedestrian safety. *(David Christie)*

Eventually facilities included a crews' mess room, cashier's office and conductors' paying-in room and enquiry and parcels office, the carriage of parcels having been a service offered by Southdown since the beginning. Parcels Agents had been established in most of the area, usually in Post Offices and village stores. In the early days a number of buses were equipped with goods compartments fitted behind the driver, primarily for the carriage of milk churns in rural areas, earning them the name of 'milk churn buses'.

The ribbon development along the coastal strip already mentioned brought increased patronage to Southdown and this was particularly true of the 'bungalow town' that had sprung up between Brighton and Newhaven. In 1916, following a competition in the national newspaper, the new town was given the name of New Anzac-on-Sea, but within a year it was changed to the idyllic-sounding name of Peacehaven. Although the Brighton to Eastbourne service had existed from the start, there was only one through journey per day, the remainder terminating at Seaford.

With the increase in traffic the service was improved with buses running regularly through to Eastbourne.

Eastbourne Corporation was already firmly established in the town, having become the world's first municipal motor bus operator in 1903, so having established a stage carriage service into the town Southdown had to look elsewhere for expansion. A route was started to Hailsham and Uckfield to the north-west where Southdown's buses met with those of the East Surrey Traction Company and Autocar of Tunbridge Wells. To the east a service to Hastings was introduced, again operated jointly with Maidstone & District in whose area it terminated.

As early as 1916 premises in Pevensey Road were leased from the Kemp Town Brewery, the freehold being purchased three years later. Again this was an example of Southdown's apparent love of difficult entrances. Buses turned from Langney Road into the entrance, immediately finding themselves in a narrow tunnel that led to the bus station proper, the exit being in Pevensey Road itself.

29

PARCELS EXPRESS DELIVERY SERVICE.

A Parcels Express Delivery Service has been established in connection with the Omnibus Service in the following districts :—Brighton, Newhaven, Seaford, Burgess Hill, Cuckfield, Ansty, Hurstpierpoint, Hassocks, Ditchling, Albourne, Keymer, Patcham, Pyecombe, Lewes, Telscombe, Rottingdean, Shoreham, Steyning, Bramber, Beeding, Beeding Cement Works, Portslade, Southwick.

Parcels will be received subject to the conditions printed below, at any of the receiving offices in the list which appears below, to be sent " carriage paid " or " carriage forward " to any of the other receiving offices at the following rates :—

Up to 7 lbs.	4d.
7–14 lbs.	6d.
14–56 lbs.	8d.

By prepayment of an additional 1d. per parcel, delivery of " carriage paid " parcels can be obtained at any point on actual route of buses, or at any point within a one-mile radius of any receiving office marked " a " in list below :—

RECEIVING OFFICES.

		OPEN a.m. p.m
ALBOURNE	King's Head Inn.	8—8
ANSTY	a. Mr. A. J. Green, Ansty Post Office.	8—8 Wed. 8—1
BRAMBER & BEEDING	T. Adams, Bridge House, Beeding.	9—7
BRIGHTON	a. Royal Mews, Steine Street. Tel., Kemp Town 1428.	8—8
	a. Central Garage, Middle Street. Tel., B'ton. 4902.	8—8
Cement Works, BEEDING	Mr. A. Simmonds, The General Stores.	9—7
CUCKFIELD	" Rose and Crown "	8—8

30

		OPEN. a.m. p.m.
HURST-PIERPOINT	Mrs. Cragg, High Street.	8—8 Wed. 8—2
LEWES	a. Messrs. Payne and Edgcombe, 5, Seveirg Buildings, High Street.	8—8
	Mr. P. D. Le Seeleur, High Street, Lewes.	8—8
NEWHAVEN	a. Old Brewery House, Bridge Street. Tel., Newhaven 42.	8—8
PATCHAM	C. J. Friend, Grocer, Patcham.	8—8 Wed. 8—1
PORTSLADE	Mr. M. J. Beadle, Wellington Road.	9—7 Wed. 9—1
ROTTING-DEAN	a. Mr. Wallace, Royal Oak Hotel.	8—8
SEAFORD	a. The Shelter, Esplanade, Seaford. Tel., Seaford 117.	8—8
SHOREHAM	Mrs. Woolmore, Norfolk Bridge, Tobacco Stores.	9—7
SOUTHWICK	Mr. A. E. Harris, The Broadway.	9—7
STEYNING	Stedham House, High Street.	8—8
TELSCOMBE	Mr. Groves, Telscombe Post Office.	8—8 Wed. 8—1

Parcels service – charges and list of Agents, 1915 *(Author's Collection)*

In 1927 a garage was opened that had been built on land bought from the Eastbourne Ice and Cold Storage Co Ltd in Royal Parade three years earlier. Initially home to Eastbourne's allocation of thirty-odd vehicles, it was later used largely for the accommodation of coaches and, rather like Park Street in Brighton, particularly for the storage of touring coaches and, prior to the introduction of convertibles, open-toppers during the winter months.

Eastbourne's second garage was originally that of Chapman & Sons but was not included in the sale when Southdown purchased that operator in 1932, being retained by Chapman for the use of visiting coaches to the town. However, following further negotiations the garage, which was situated between Susan's Road and Cavendish Place, was bought outright by Southdown the following year. As well as providing further garage accommodation, the complex also became Eastbourne's Coach Station.

Most of the operators acquired during the 1920s were engaged in excursion and tours work but two in the Eastbourne area were stage carriage operators. One was T A Piper's 'Red Saloon Motor Services' of Hellingly, which operated a service from its home village to Eastbourne, the other H J Twine of Polegate who ran services from Eastbourne to Jevington and to Polegate Station, which Southdown numbered 93 and 93B respectively. Twine's business brought with it four fairly new single-deckers; two Thornycrofts, a Graham Dodge and a Dennis E. Following their withdrawal in 1931 the two Thornycrofts were sold to Denmead Queen only to find themselves returning to the Southdown fleet in 1935 with the purchase of Denmead Queen.

Following the purchase of George Town's local services in 1919 Southdown had established a virtual monopoly in the town and, as it had in Eastbourne it began to look further afield for opportunities to expand. The frontline service 31 from Brighton to Portsmouth passed through the town, of course and the establishment of services to Horsham from both Worthing and Brighton resulted in the opening of a garage in that town in 1919. The first of two garages in Dane Road was bought in 1924, a second being acquired in 1935. After much extension and enlargement the garage eventually housed some 50 vehicles. The garage closed in 1987 becoming a store for vehicles awaiting sale and a magnet for enthusiasts!

Like Uckfield, Horsham was one of the boundary towns where Southdown vehicles met with those of London Transport (originally East Surrey), Aldershot & District, Hants & Sussex and a host of smaller independents.

A service from Littlehampton to Arundel and Angmering was acquired with the purchase of the South Coast Touring Company of Littlehampton in 1924. Also included was an office in Beach Road together with six charabancs and two single-deck buses, all but one being of Dennis manufacture and the first of this make to enter the Southdown fleet. The odd one out was one of the few AECs to be operated by Southdown. The office served the company until 1926 when a garage was opened in East Street, which grew over the years both in its vehicle allocation and the amount of traffic handled, eventually becoming the town's bus and coach station.

The Bognor and Chichester areas expanded largely through acquisition. Mention has already been made of the purchase of

The Parcels Service was an important part of Southdown's operations, offering a much faster delivery time than the Royal Mail, providing the recipient was prepared to call at the nearest agent to collect the package. It was a service that was advertised widely by the company as illustrated by this leaflet, which included a fine illustration of a Leyland TD double-decker complete with full nearside destination display. *(Michael Rooum Collection)*

the Arthur Davies' business in Bognor before Southdown was even properly established. Davies was made Area Manager and Bognor became the focal point for services between Worthing and Portsmouth. In 1920 a service was started between Chichester and Selsey using double-deckers on a two-hourly frequency, a service that proved so popular the competing railway service was forced to close in 1935 Colonel Stephens' West Sussex Railway operated under the delightful name of 'The Hundred Manhood and Selsey

Tramway', the name being chosen to avoid having to adhere to railway regulations. Like some other Col. Stephens railways, the motive power was provided by Railmotors, one pair made by Shefflex Motors of Sheffield, a lorry manufacturer; another pair were based on Model 'T' Ford chassis and a final pair consisted of a Wolseley-Siddeley car conversion coupled to a Ford 'T' lorry. Fascinating stuff indeed! The line suffered severe flood damage in 1911 from which the company never really recovered financially and the competition from Southdown hammered the final nail into its coffin.

1923 saw the business of A E Trickey of Birdham acquired with a service to West Wittering while later that year the purchase of Royal Blue Bus Services of Bognor gave Southdown a local Bognor service from Aldwick to Middleton together with three Guy and three Ford buses. Next to succumb was Summersdale Motor Services of Chichester, which operated a stage carriage service between Chichester and Pagham, the Southdown fleet gaining two more Vulcans, this time with bus bodies by Cutten together with a Model T Ford 14-seater. April 1924 saw the introduction of service 39 (later renumbered 60) from Bognor to Petersfield via Chichester and Midhurst. Midhurst was roughly the half-way point and a temporary garage was rented in the town, more permanent accommodation being built a couple of years later.

Over the years operating importance moved from Bognor to Chichester and two garages in Northgate were opened in the 1920s, both of which had entertainment connections, one being built on the site of the Olympic Picture House, the other on what was the local ice rink. In the absence of a bus station buses congregated around the cathedral, which did not meet with the approval of local residents. Even so it was not until 1956 that a purpose-built garage and bus station was opened in Southgate, beside the railway line.

Eastbourne's Royal Parade garage was ideally situated on the sea front and in latter years was used mainly for the accommodation of coaches as illustrated by this October 1967 view showing, inside the garage, three Leyland Leopards with Harrington Cavalier bodies and, parked outside, a Weymann Fanfare-bodied Leyland Tiger Cub. All have cream relief making what was probably Southdown's most attractive coach livery. *(Southdown Enthusiasts' Club)*

The business side of Eastbourne's Pevensey Road bus station on a busy summer's day in July 1968. Visible in this view are, from left to right, a Southdown open-top Guy on the Beachy Head service, a Maidstone & District AEC Regent V on the jointly operated service 15 to Hastings and a Southdown Leyland PD2/12 working the 190. Note the white summer covers on the crews' caps. *(Southdown Enthusiasts' Club)*

Another entrance to test drivers' skills was that of the Pevensey Road Bus Station in Eastbourne. Here a Maidstone & District lowbridge Atlantean squeezes into the Langney Road entrance and the narrow tunnel. *(John Short/Alan Lambert Collection)*

Expansion in the Portsmouth area was rapid. Mention has already been made of Frank Bartlett who, after his association with Worthing Motor Services, was put in charge of Portsmouth operations. Following the re-introduction of Mackenzie's Portsmouth service, Bartlett showed great initiative by arranging for buses on layover at Bognor to be sent on to Portsmouth where he filled them with excursion passengers at five shillings (25p) and sent them on a trip back to Bognor!

In 1921 Southdown inaugurated a service to Fareham to connect with Hants & Dorset buses to Southampton. In the following year a joint service was introduced operated by Southdown and Hants & Dorset over the whole route from Portsmouth to Southampton whilst a second joint service took Southdown vehicles further into Hampshire as far as Winchester. However, in 1925 boundaries were re-drawn and both Hants & Dorset and Southdown retreated to their former terminus at Fareham.

More locally, traffic increased with families wanting to ride out into the surrounding countryside, while in the opposite direction

Cavendish Place Coach Station Booking Office was, like Bognor Bus Station, a fine example of 1930s Art Deco style of building. Unfortunately its architectural value did not save it from being demolished to make way for flats and houses. *(John Short/Alan Lambert Collection)*

Even the then small market town of Hailsham warranted a smart and stylish Booking Office. *(Ian Richardson Collection)*

Horsham Enquiry and Booking Office at 23 The Carfax, opened in 1933, was modernised in 1958. Horsham was one of the 'border' towns between Southdown and London Transport areas, hence the LT bulls-eye on the fascia. *(Southdown Chronicle/Stagecoach South)*

Littlehampton's allocation of vehicles grew steadily over the years, as did the traffic it handled, particularly on the coaching side. By the time this photograph was taken in the sixties it had earned itself the title of 'Bus and Coach Station' and had a thriving Booking and Enquiry Office. The Leyland PD3 is departing for Brighton on service 31. *(Southdown Enthusiasts' Club)*

Midhurst depot was opened in 1924 to service route 39 (later 60) from Bognor to Petersfield. The original rented wooden building was replaced by a more permanent structure a couple of years later. Midhurst was yet another example of Southdown's apparent love of 'tight fits' as demonstrated by all-Leyland PD2 382 (JCD 82) as it squeezes its way out of the garage. *(Paul Haywood)*

There were two variations of route for the express service from London to Littlehampton, which were operated on a roughly alternate basis, one running via Redhill and Crawley, the other via Kingston and Dorking, a common route being maintained from Horsham onwards This May 1955 timetable leaflet features one of the Leyland-bodied Royal Tiger coaches that were the mainstay of Southdown's express services throughout the early fifties. *(Howard Butler Collection)*

Southdown
MOTOR SERVICES LIMITED

EXPRESS COACH SERVICE

BETWEEN

London, Worthing and Littlehampton

via Dorking or Redhill

TIME TABLE AND FARE TABLE

Winter Period from 27th September, 1954 until 25th May, 1955

BOOK YOUR SEAT AT :

LONDON SERVICE LEAFLET No. 4D 1954/3/30m

came passengers wishing to sample the delights of the increasingly popular electric cinema. An even stronger foothold was gained in the City with the acquisition of the Southsea Tourist Company, which operated in competition with the Portsdown & Horndean Light Railway, with some journeys running beyond Horndean as far as Petersfield. The Southsea Tourist Company also operated a service within the City boundaries from Clarence Pier to Stubbington Road via Eastney and Milton. Concerned about the increasing competition the Corporation decreed that Southdown should charge a minimum fare of 6d (2½p) on its services. This was later relaxed, Southdown being required to pay a protective fare of around 2d (1p) above the Corporation fare.

Throughout the 'twenties and 'thirties there were many more acquisitions both in the Portsmouth area, and indeed throughout Southdown's territory, far too numerous to mention here. However, by 1934 Southdown was running from South Parade Pier to Emsworth, Fareham, Hayling Island, Horndean, Petersfield, South Harting, Warsash and Westbourne as well as locally between North End and the Dockyard, these all in spite of objections from the Corporation. There were many agreements and protective fare arrangements over the years, but it was not until 1946 that a proper co-ordination scheme was introduced.

In 1919 a booking office had been opened at Frank Bartlett's premises in Southsea, but the first garage to serve the Portsmouth area was opened in 1922 at Emsworth. The first garage in Portsmouth proper opened in 1923 at Hyde Park Road, on the site of a women's prison. The premises were extended and developed considerably over the ensuing years.

The smart modern frontage of the west side of Chichester Bus Station. *(Southdown Enthusiasts' Club)*

An abridged pre-war map showing the main bus routes that formed the basic network of Southdown's stage carriage services. *(Capital Transport Collection)*

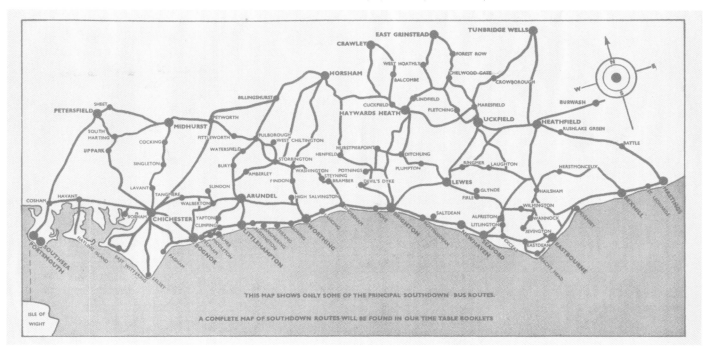

THIS MAP SHOWS ONLY SOME OF THE PRINCIPAL SOUTHDOWN BUS ROUTES.

A COMPLETE MAP OF SOUTHDOWN ROUTES WILL BE FOUND IN OUR TIME TABLE BOOKLETS

1933 saw the formation of the London Passenger Transport Board, which took control of most of the operators in London and its surrounding countryside. The board re-drew its boundaries and, in Sussex, retreated to East Grinstead, leaving Southdown free to extend its Eastbourne – Uckfield service northward to the new 'border town'. Other services in the area passed to Maidstone & District. Southdown 658 (UF 4658), a 1929 Tilling-Stevens B10A2 with 31-seat Short Bros body heads for Eastbourne on the lengthened route. Note the black-on-white destination blind, with the route number in more usual white-on-black, a Southdown feature of this time. *(The Omnibus Society)*

By 1934 the fleet had grown considerably by acquisition and competition and a new and impressive bus garage and coach station was built in Hilsea, at the northern end of Portsea Island. Like Hyde Park Road it was developed and extended, eventually becoming Southdown's largest garage.

Around the turn of the decade there were several important developments, both locally and nationally, which affected the future of Southdown. In January 1926, following the death of Flexman French, Sidney Garcke was appointed Chairman of Southdown. Garcke's father had been the founder of the British Electric Traction Company. And Garcke himself had been Managing Director by the British Automobile Traction Company, of which Southdown was an associated company. This volume is not the place to go into the politics of the bus industry, suffice to say that in 1928 the British Automobile Traction Company joined forces with Thomas Tilling to form Tilling-BAT, of which Southdown was again a member. 1942 saw Tilling-BAT divided into two groups, Tilling and the British Electric Traction Co, the two groups between them managing the majority of the larger non-municipal operators. Southdown, not surprisingly, found itself under B.E.T control.

The next major development was the implementation of the 1930 Road Traffic Act under which all crews, vehicles and services were required to be licensed. As far as services were concerned applications had to be made to the Traffic Commissioner and there was an opportunity for any other operator, including the railways, to object if they felt their own services would suffer as a result. The Act brought about the end of much unfair, unregulated and wasteful competition.

Operationally, the most important development as far as Southdown was concerned was probably the introduction of the Leyland Titan TD1 double-deck chassis and its single-deck counterpart, the TS1 Tiger. The TD1, introduced at the 1927 Commercial Motor Show was fitted with a 6-cylinder engine, employed vacuum brakes and, possibly most important of all, a low height chassis frame that allowed the fitting of a covered top deck. It set the scene for the future, the Titan in its various forms becoming the standard double-decker for some forty years.

Thus the scene was set. The Southdown map had been drawn and, with one or two minor exceptions, was to remain the same until the birth of the National Bus Company.

'Keeping the Wheels Turning'

In 1928 Southdown opened its new Central Works at Victoria Road, Portslade. Extended and updated over the years it was able to deal with most of the Company's engineering and bodywork maintenance and repairs needed to uphold its extremely high standards. This view of the imposing frontage was taken in 1962. *(Southdown Enthusiasts' Club)*

Southdown was justifiably proud of its ancillary fleet as well as its buses and coaches and this photo of new Ford service vehicles appeared in a 1962 issue of the Southdown Chronicle. *(Southdown Chronicle/Stagecoach South)*

'Enter the Titan'

Although the low frame of the Leyland Titan allowed for an enclosed upper deck, Southdown's first examples delivered in 1929 were fitted with 51-seat open top, open-staircase bodies built by Brush of Loughborough. These three official photographs by the bodybuilder show the nearside, rear and offside of number 804 (UF 4804) *(Brush Archives/S J Butler Collection)*

806 (UF 4806) stands on Worthing sea front with blinds set for the return journey to Brighton on what would appear to be a sunny if somewhat windy day, judging by the lady holding on to her hat and the lack of passengers on the upper deck. *(W J Haynes/Southdown Enthusiasts' Club)*

The next two batches of TD1s had Leyland's own bodywork, including both low- and highbridge versions. 868 (UF 6468) was one of the full-height versions with 48-seat bodywork, and is seen at High Salvington. *(Glyn Kraemer-Johnson Collection)*

One of these buses, 873 (UF 6473), has been preserved and is in the safe hands of the Amberley Working Museum. It is seen here 'in service' at a Worthing Running Day on 24th July 2004. *(Glyn Kraemer-Johnson)*

The final two batches of TD1s, totalling no fewer than 55 in number, carried bodies by Short Bros of Rochester, the first five seating 48, the remainder 50. The Short Bros body had a more modern appearance than the Leyland product with, apart from the vee-shaped front upper-deck windows, a fairly smooth frontal profile and less of the 'piano front' effect of Leyland's version. Again thanks to the efforts of the Amberley Working Museum a Short-bodied TD1 survives for us to enjoy. 948 (UF 7428) was photographed with blinds and destination boards set for trunk route 31, on which it would have worked when new. *(Southdown Enthusiasts' Club)*

The coaching side – Excursions, Tours and Express Services

Excursions and tours had played an important part in Southdown's operations right from the very beginning with Mackenzie's day trips to Ascot and Epsom Races and tours to Cornwall, Wales and the Lake District, not to mention Mantell's horse-drawn charabanc excursions from Brighton Sea Front to Devil's Dyke, and would continue to do so until the desecration of the coach fleet by Stage-coach.

Unfortunately, at the time of Southdown's formation in 1915 the First World War prevented travel for pleasure and following the Armistice what vehicles that could be obtained were sorely needed for stage carriage work

However, with a number of major holiday resorts in its area, excursion work in particular was to become an important part of the Company's operations. Following the acquisition of Arthur Davies's company, together with its excursion licences, Southdown maintained a stronghold in this field, largely by acquisition, most of the companies bought being engaged in coaching rather than bus work. In the west of the area Southdown's position was strengthened considerably by the purchase of South Coast Tourist of Littlehampton in 1924 and its sister company the Southsea Tourist Co Ltd in the following year.

A couple of experimental tours had been operated in 1922 and 1923 but it was the acquisition of the Southsea Tourist Company with its established programme of tours that enabled Mackenzie to fulfil his dream and resurrect his own programme of 'coach cruises' as they were always known by Southdown. Thus, in 1926 he introduced a full programme of coach holidays ranging from three to ten days in duration.

To the east of the area, companies purchased included Royal Red of Hove, Potts of Brighton and Cavendish Coaches of Eastbourne. Also in Eastbourne was the largest of Southdown's acquisitions, this being Chapman and Sons, purchased in 1932 and bringing with it some 50 vehicles as well as premises in the Eastbourne area. Chapman operated tours not only in Great Britain and Ireland, but to France, Switzerland and Italy. By 1934 these acquisitions had put Southdown in the forefront of tour operators in the UK, its coach cruises covering the whole of Great Britain.

An early tours brochure showing no fewer than thirteen departures during September – including 17 days in the Scottish Highlands for £28.15.0d *(Howard Butler Collection)*

Right 1930 tours brochure (front) *(Michael Rooum Collection)*

Far right 1930 tours brochure (back) *(Michael Rooum Collection)*

RAYMOND PERCIVAL BEDDOW

Raymond Percival Beddow received a public school education at Mill Hill, a school popular with commercial and businessmen. At the age of 20 he applied to join the British Electric Traction Co but, although he was described as well-dressed, personable and well-spoken, his appointment was by no means a foregone conclusion. He had to undergo three extremely tough interviews before he was eventually accepted. He was appointed as personal assistant to Mr Shirreff Hilton, a member of the board and chairman of a number of B.E.T.'s associated companies.

Just a year later he was appointed assistant secretary of the Shropshire, Worcestershire and Staffordshire Electric Power Co, B.E.T.'s biggest electricity supply subsidiary, and two years after that he became secretary. The Shropshire company passed out of

B.E.T.'s hands during the 1930s, but Beddow had proved his worth and within two years he was secretary of East Midland and Trent. By 1937 he had become secretary of B.E.T. itself.

In the early years of the war Beddow had the task of organising B.E.T. headquarters, dealing with evacuation, air raids and the mobilisation of virtually the entire workforce and was also very much involved in the affairs of a number of bus companies including City of Oxford, East Kent, Maidstone & District and Southdown together with London Coastal Coaches, all of which he became Chairman of. He was appointed as Chairman of Southdown in May 1946 and held that position until the Transport Holding Company took control in 1968; a quite remarkable record. He was awarded the CBE in 1956.

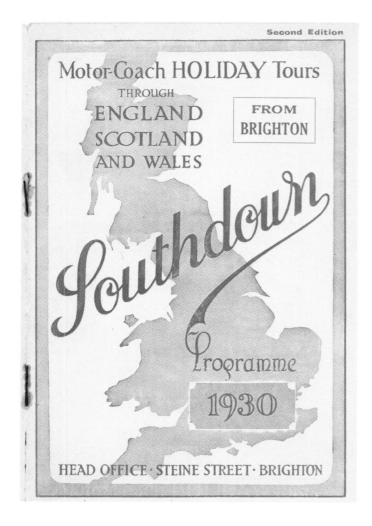

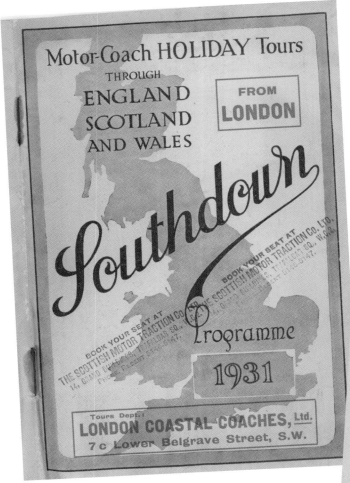

Early co-ordination. 1931 Tours brochure distributed by London Coastal Coaches Ltd and stamped inside to the effect that seats may be booked at 'Scottish Motor Traction Ltd, Grand Buildings, Trafalgar Square'. The itinerary and map are for the twelve day tour to the Lake District and Scotland, which must have been quite an adventure at the time. *(Michael Rooum Collection)*

'THE TOURERS'

While the charabanc reigned supreme throughout the 1920s, experiments were being made with armchair-type seating and central gangways that allowed a single entrance instead of separate doors to each row of seats. Experiments were also carried out with removable celluloid side windows, but these were not altogether successful. However, between 1930 and 1933, following on from these experiments, Southdown took delivery of seventeen touring coaches on Leyland Lioness LTB1 normal control chassis and fitted with Harrington C20R bodies. The height of luxury for their time, their 20 seats were arranged in rows of three with pairs of seats on the offside of the gangway and single seats on the nearside, an arrangement Southdown was to perpetuate on its touring coaches until NBC days. The company remained faithful to the normal control chassis for its touring coaches and in 1936 took delivery of six Leyland Tigress LTB3 chassis with Burlingham bodies, the last tourers to be received before the outbreak of World War II.

Southdown made no secret of the fact that it regarded its coach cruises as being for the 'upper end of the market' aimed at passengers with a certain standing and respectability, hence its higher-than-average prices. Its excursion programme however was intended for the day tripper and holiday maker, who having had their fill of cockles and whelks and a glass of brown ale, would take a trip to Devil's Dyke, Beachy Head or the Meon Valley. The local populace, who enjoyed a day at the races, were catered for and excursions to Goodwood, Fontwell and Lingfield as well as Epsom and Ascot remained popular until largely killed off by the private car.

Excursions had been an important part of the company's activities from the very start although, as with the extended tours, the First World War had brought such operations to a halt. After the Armistice they expanded rapidly, again largely through acquisition. Vehicles would line the sea fronts each morning with excursion details beautifully written with coloured chalks on blackboards leaning against them. Drivers would wait beside their vehicles waiting for bookings and it has to be said that Southdown drivers were less persistent and aggravating in their attempts to drum up business than those of the competing independent operators.

Both coach cruises and excursions continued to expand throughout the 1930s and, with growing tension in Europe encouraging people to holiday in Britain, 1939 proved to be Southdown's most successful season. However, all that was to end in September of that year with Britain's declaration of war on Germany. The south coast became a restricted area and the holiday traffic disappeared almost overnight.

Alongside its coach cruises, excursions and private hire operations, Southdown had been steadily extending and expanding its network of express services.

There is no doubt that express services would have become a part of Southdown's operations in due course, but in the event their introduction was brought about by circumstances beyond the company's control. In 1919 a rail strike was called by the NUR as a result of which Chapman's of Eastbourne started a rescue service, carrying stranded holidaymakers back to London. When, after eleven days the strike came to an end Chapman and a number of other operators continued to run what soon became profitable services from Brighton and Eastbourne to the capital, Southdown could not afford to miss out on the opportunity and in 1920 was one of nine operators which formed London & Coast Coaches to pool their interests. Competition continued to increase and in 1925 London Coastal Coaches Ltd was established, its aim being to apportion mileage, to regularise fares and timings and most importantly to find off-street parking for the many coaches arriving daily in the capital. The first such place was a muddy two-acre site in Lupus Street, near Vauxhall Bridge. Opened in April 1928, the Easter weekend of that year saw some 1,250 departures to all parts of the country. Hardly ideal, the coach station offered no shelter for passengers and had only one narrow road that acted as entrance and exit for both coaches and pedestrians.

At the other end of its area, Southdown had acquired a number of operators with licences for express services on the Portsmouth to London Road. One particularly worthy of mention was 'Underwood Express', which operated a service from King's Cross to Southsea where passengers were allowed eleven and a half hours before making the return journey. To capitalise on this free time, Underwood organised a connecting air service from Southsea to Ryde in conjunction with the Isle of Wight Aviation Company. At the time of Southdown's take-over, negotiations were under way for a coach-air service to Jersey, something which was later to be introduced by Southdown.

With further acquisitions, services eventually spread fan-like from London to Warsash in the west and Eastbourne. The service to Gosport and Fareham was of interest, terminating as it did in Hants & Dorset territory. This came about because of an agree-

The inside of the 1931 tour brochure featured a photograph of a magnificent Leyland LTB1 'Lioness' with Harrington 20-seat body. The vehicle featured is number 307 (UF 6507) of the second batch and is shown in original condition with canvas roof. (Michael Rooum Collection)

BOOK YOUR SEAT AT
THE SCOTTISH MOTOR TRACTION Co. Ltd.
149 GRAND BUILDINGS, TRAFALGAR SQ., W.C.2.
PHONE. REGENT 5140-5147.

SOUTHDOWN MOTOR SERVICES, Ltd.

Programme of Motor Coach
Holiday Tours, 1931

The Itineraries given are liable to slight alteration.
Night Accommodation is provided at the Hotels enclosed in brackets.

THESE TOURS LEAVE FROM
——AND RETURN TO——
7c LOWER BELGRAVE STREET
VICTORIA : LONDON
S.W.

ment between Hants & Dorset and Royal Blue to the effect that the former would not operate express services, thus the way was left clear for Southdown.

The base line of the triangle was completed in 1929 when Southdown introduced its South Coast Express service operated jointly with East Kent and Wilts & Dorset between Margate and Bournemouth, a service already being operated by Elliott Bros 'Royal Blue' company. Following acute competition, agreement was reached in 1932 whereby Southdown and East Kent coaches terminated at Southdown's Hyde Park Road depot, Portsmouth, passengers wishing to continue their journey westwards transferring at this point to a Royal Blue vehicle, Royal Blue having taken over Wilts & Dorset's share of the service.

Refreshment stops on express services had been made at various hostelries *en route*, but such was the traffic on the Worthing and Brighton to London services that in 1931 Southdown opened its County Oak coach station, a 'halfway house' stopping point that offered toilet and refreshment facilities.

A year later, London Coastal Coaches opened its new 'art deco' Victoria Coach Station in Buckingham Palace Road, London, a site which it still occupies today.

In 1938/39 these coaches were updated by Harrington which fitted them with fixed roofs incorporating a central sliding section and glass cant panels to preserve the passengers' upward view, another feature that was perpetuated by Southdown on its touring coaches for many years. 316 (UF 8830) of 1933 is seen at Victoria Coach Station thus modified. In 1948 this particular vehicle was rebuilt by Windover, receiving a central entrance. (*Omnibus Society*)

At the opposite end of the country, car 318 was photographed at Looe in Cornwall while on a coach cruise to Devon and Cornwall, the work for which it was intended. *(Alan Cross)*

Burlingham-bodied Leyland Tigress 323 (CUF 323) *(From a painting by John Kinsley/Transport Art Collections)*

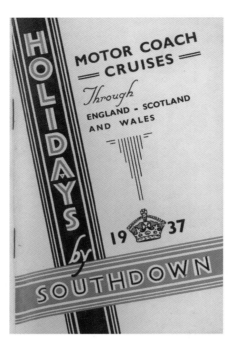

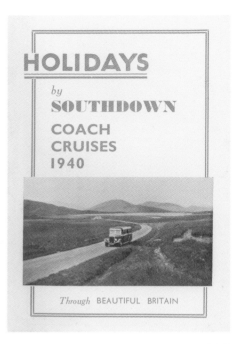

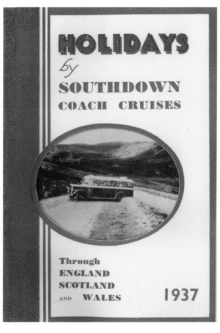

Two brochures were issued in 1937. The cover of the first commemorated the coronation of HM King George VI and included the usual picture of a Lioness inside. The cover of the second was to a new design and featured one of the Leyland Tigress coaches delivered the previous year. *(Michael Rooum Collection)*

The Tigress appeared again on the inside page of the 1939 brochure and on the cover of the 1940 programme, although the outbreak of war would undoubtedly meant that the latter programme was cancelled. *(Michael Rooum Collection)*

By 1930 a full programme of day, half-day and evening excursions was being offered. The brochure for July of that year features a typical Tilling Stevens with canvas roof. *(Michael Rooum Collection)*

1135 (CCD 735), a 1936 Leyland TS7 with 32-seat bodywork by Beadle of Dartford, on an excursion to the Dicker Pottery. Situated on the main A22 between Hailsham and Uckfield, the Pottery, which dated back to the mid-nineteenth century, closed in 1956. *(Omnibus Society)*

The Leyland Cub was a versatile little vehicle, being used by Southdown for coach cruises, excursions, express, private hire and stage carriage work. Number 41 (DUF 41) was a KPZ2 delivered in 1937 with 20-seat Harrington bodywork. It is seen waiting to depart on an excursion to Selsey Bill. *(Omnibus Society)*

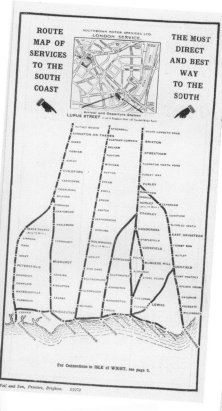

Express Service leaflets: 1929-30

London to the South Coast Express Services timetable, dated April 1930 *(Howard Butler Collection)*

1930 map of express services from London to the South Coast, also showing the location of the Lupus Street Coach Station. *(Howard Butler Collection)*

London to Isle of Wight express timetable September 1929. *(Howard Butler Collection)*

1929 London to Brighton Express service fare and Timetable leaflet, offering an increased daily service, six journeys a day from Great Scotland Yard and Lupus Street. 'Travel by the famous green coaches, all equipped with interior electric lighting, floor mats and rugs.' *(Howard Butler Collection)*

The crew pose in front of the coach featured on the 1931 and 1932 express leaflets, Leyland TS2 1044 (UF 7344) taking a break at the recently opened Crawley Coach Station. *(Arthur Ingram)*

The following pictures were taken from the March 1957 issue of the Southdown Chronicle, published to mark the 25th Anniversary of Victoria Coach Station.

A 1950s view showing the imposing frontage of Victoria Coach Station. *(Southdown Chronicle/Stagecoach South)*

'Happy Holiday! Friends and relatives wave goodbye to passengers on a coach leaving Victoria for Eastbourne. *(Southdown Chronicle/Stagecoach South)*

The first Southdown vehicle to enter the new coach station was 202 (UF 8302), one of three TSM C60A7s with Harrington coachwork, new in 1931. TSM was the trading name of the Maidstone company following its separation from the Tilling Group in 1930. The old Tilling Stevens 'birdcage' radiator grille had been replaced by a new design resembling that of Leyland. *(Southdown Chronicle/Stagecoach South)*

Express Services leaflets 1933-1939

Competition on the Portsmouth road in 1933/4 from Timpson's 'Solent Line Coaches' whose AEC coach was shown on the front of its timetable for the winter period. Timpson surrendered its licence for this service in 1935. *(Michael Rooum Collection)*

Old faithful! Although by then four years old, TS2 1044 reappeared on the 1935 timetable for the Gosport service, which claimed to incorporate the 'Perseverance' express coach service, a company that had been acquired by Southdown in July 1934. *(Michael Rooum Collection)*

The Coronation of His Majesty King George VI warranted extra and later journeys into and out of London and also justified a special commemorative time table leaflet. *(Michael Rooum Collection)*

Lewes, Newhaven and Eastbourne express services 1937. *(Michael Rooum Collection)*

By 1939 the Leyland Tiger was well established and featured on the front of that year's London – Brighton timetable. 'Every hour on the hour' was true enough at the start of the timetable period, but a week before its expiry war had been declared and services would soon see severe reductions. *(Michael Rooum Collection)*

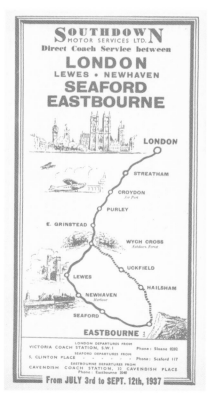

Typifying the Southdown coach of the 1930s is preserved 1179 (DUF 179), a 1937 Leyland TS7 with Harrington 32-seat body. The pictures of this superbly preserved vehicle show the restrained elegance of the styling and livery and the luxurious air of the interior.
(Mervyn Stedman)

On Stage – The stage-carriage fleet in the 1930s

As with the previous Titans, the TD5s were fitted with a mixture of high- and lowbridge bodies. The 1938 EUF-registered batch consisted of no fewer than 51 vehicles, all of which were mounted with lowbridge bodies by either Park Royal or Beadle. This rare colour shot shows 192 (EUF 192) with the Beadle version. The Brighton Corporation tram in the background dates the photo to pre-mid 1939. *(Geoffrey Morant)*

Numerically the very last pre-war double-decker delivered to Southdown was 265 (GCD 365) with lowbridge Park Royal bodywork, identifiable by the heavily radiused lower corners to the front side windows. A further 27 double-deckers were on order at this time being Leyland TD7s, again with lowbridge Park Royal bodies. However, following the outbreak of the Second World War they were diverted to Western Welsh (7), Crosville (16) and Cumberland Motor Services (4). *(W J Haynes/Southdown Enthusiasts' Club)*

The Leyland Tiger saloon did not have the same immediate impact on the stage-carriage fleet as had its double-deck counterpart. Between 1928 and 1931 the Company had bought more than 100 Tilling Stevens B10A2 chassis, their rear entrance bus bodywork being shared largely between Short Bros and Harrington. Amongst the first batch to be delivered in 1928 was number 472 (UF 3072) with 32-seat Short Bros body. By the time this photograph was taken it had been renumbered 612 and was working the scenic 26A service from Eastbourne to Seaford via High and Over. The bus had an interesting afterlife, being withdrawn by Southdown in 1939 and sold to the Elephant & Castle Horse Repository, holders of the largest weekly auction of horses in the country. What use was found for 612 is a matter for conjecture. *(Southdown Enthusiasts' Club)*

Many of the vehicles acquired with the purchase of other operators were of the smaller, low capacity types suitable for the more rural and less patronised services. Many were of Dennis manufacture and the reliability of the type prompted Southdown to purchase twenty-six new Dennis 30 cwt chassis in 1926/7. All but two were fitted with Short Bros bodies of 19-seat capacity, of which 517 (UF 1517) was one, being new in 1927. Withdrawn in 1932, it was sold to the Shoreham Shipping & Coal Company for use as a lorry before being rescued by the Amberley Working Museum and restored to its original condition. It is seen here passing through Shoreham during a commemorative road run in 2004. *(Glyn Kraemer-Johnson)*

For its next generation of small single-deckers Southdown turned to the Leyland Cub KPZ, a type that had already proved its versatility in the coaching field. Fourteen were delivered during 1936-37, all with 20-seat bodies by Park Royal. 21 (ECD 521) was one of the final batch dating from 1937 and is seen at Horsham Carfax in original pre-war livery. The Horsham local services were amongst the regular haunts of these useful little buses. (*Omnibus Society*)

One of the more unusual purchases was the fleet of Tramocar of Worthing, which was acquired by Southdown in 1938. Tramocar operated a fleet of Shelvoke & Drewry 'Freighters' with tiller steering and small wheels, the latter allowing for a low floor that was ideally suited to the largely elderly residents of Worthing. Passing the Worthing Dome is T3 (PX 886), the oldest of the eleven taken over, having been built in 1924. It is wearing the red and white 'Tramocar' livery that they retained until withdrawal which, in the case of T3, was just four months after acquisition by Southdown. (*From a painting by Glyn Kraemer-Johnson*)

Worting sea front on Jubilee weekend 1935. In evidence are Tramocar PO 1748 and another. *(Stephen Howarth)*

Much more bus-like were the final two 'Freighters', delivered in 1938. Ordered by Tramocar they were delivered to Southdown in full green and cream livery but retaining 'Tramocar' fleetnames on the front dash. Numbered T16/17 (FCD 16/17) they had Harrington centre-entrance bodies that bore some resemblance to that company's bodies built on the AEC 'Q' side-engined chassis. Note the 'T' prefix to the route number on T16 seen at the terminus with one of the earlier versions behind. All the 'Freighters' were withdrawn by 1942, including T16/17, which had seen a mere four years' service. T16 went on to end its days as a caravan. *(Glyn Kraemer-Johnson Collection)*

Against all Odds – 1939-1945

The Second World War was not a time when style was of paramount importance but, even so, Southdown managed to maintain standards as far as, and possibly beyond, what could be expected at such a time.

The South Coast was, of course virtually in the front line and, because of the threat of invasion, much of Southdown's territory was designated a restricted area. On the beaches barbed wire, concrete blocks and land mines were used in an effort to prevent enemy landings, whilst sections were cut from the piers to the same end. Needless to say the day-trippers and holidaymakers disappeared overnight and this, together with the restriction of petrol supplies for essential use only, saw a drastic reduction in the Company's excursion trade. Southdown's coach cruises had ceased at the outbreak of hostilities but excursion and private hire operations lingered on until tighter regulations on the availability of fuel for non-essential use brought them to an end in the summer of 1941. Express services continued, albeit on a reduced timetable, but by 1942 air raids, the blackout, slogans such as 'Is your journey really necessary' and further restrictions on petrol supplies brought the network to a virtual standstill and, as has already been noted Victoria Coach Station was taken over by the War Office for the duration.

Blackout regulations included the fitting of headlamp masks, allowing little more than a pinprick of light to show through. To compensate to some small extent, the edges of the front mudguards, lifeguards and platform were painted white. Livery variations were introduced in an attempt to make vehicles less conspicuous from the air. Single-deckers had their roofs repainted dark green, something that was to be perpetuated after the war. Some double-deckers were similarly treated while others received various applications of grey and green. As can be imagined driving in the blackout was both difficult and hazardous, well-known landmarks not being visible in the unbroken darkness and many signposts having been removed. The conductors' task was little better and many used torches to try and ensure that the right fares were collected and the correct change given. Although they carried fewer passengers, the driver/conductors of one-man single-deckers had the worst of both worlds.

As with most industries the number of men called-up for military service left the workforce sadly depleted in all areas. To help cope with the shortage of conductors and drivers it was decided that women should be employed as conductresses, or 'clippies' as they became known.

The steady fleet replacement and renewal that had taken place during the 'thirties stood the company in good stead and it entered the war with a comparatively modern and well-maintained fleet, the majority of vehicles being less than ten years old.

By the end of 1939 most of the closed top TD1s of 1929/30/31 had been withdrawn, only a handful remaining to be rebodied by Park Royal in 1943. Many went to Scottish operators while, shortly after the outbreak of war, 48 of them were transferred to sister company Wilts & Dorset, which was in dire need of additional vehicles to provide transport of military and civilian personnel to Salisbury Plain and Blandford Camp. This left Southdown itself with a shortage of vehicles and, as a result, the Brush-bodied open-top open-staircase TD1s of 1929 were denied their winter hibernation and were given temporary canvas top covers, which though ungainly and probably uncomfortable nevertheless enabled them to operate throughout the year. Many, having been returned to open-top configuration, continued in service into the fifties.

Bus production had largely ceased in 1939, the manufacturers of tanks, military vehicles, aircraft, guns and warships naturally having priority. By mid-1941 operators were beginning to have difficulty in maintaining services due to lack of spare parts and skilled labour, often aggravated by bombing raids and consequent damage to vehicles. It was realised that public transport must be given increased priority if anything like normal life should continue and, more importantly, that workers were transported to and from the factories. The sudden halt in production had resulted in manufacturers being left with half-completed chassis and stocks of unused parts, the use of which was 'frozen' by the Government. The Ministry of Supply therefore ordered the release of these items and that as many buses as possible should be completed. In a second initiative the Ministry of War Transport raised the maximum capacity of single-deckers to 60, these to be accommodated on seats arranged around the perimeter of the bus, with a central area available for standees.

Southdown took advantage of this relaxation and between 1941 and 1943 a large number of the 1400-class Leyland TS7 and TS8 single-deckers were thus converted. The seating capacity was reduced from 32 to 30, the seats being repositioned around the

In December 1939 Southdown introduced revised timetables for its London express services. The Brighton service was reduced to six journeys per day, the others being cut to just three. By 1942 tighter fuel restrictions, more emphasis on essential services and the public's encouragement to travel only when absolutely necessary brought about the virtual abandonment of the Company's express network. *(Howard Butler Collection)*

Strangely, when most of the fleet was receiving 'camouflage' liveries, 807 (UF 4807) received its dark green top cover but retained its largely cream open-top livery. This view shows how the canvas was stretched over and fixed to the upper deck panelling. *(Omnibus Society)*

Interior of the upper deck on one of the converted TD1s. The front and front side windows were of glass while the remainder were celluloid. *(Omnibus Society)*

sides of the bus, leaving space in the central area for 30 standing passengers. Whilst the arrangement allowed for an additional 28 passengers to be carried, it also made the conductor's task even more difficult, especially at night. All were returned to their original layout between 1945 and 1948.

Following the bombing of Pearl Harbour and America's entry into the conflict at the end of 1941, the tide of the war appeared to be turning. In 1942, when all eyes were on El Alamein, the Pacific and the Germans' advance on Russia, an almost unnoticed event was taking place, which was to have a far-reaching effect on the British bus industry. In June of that year the directors of the two parent companies decided that greater efficiency would be achieved if the business of Tilling and British Automobile Traction Ltd were divided into two parts. The result of this was the formation of two companies, the B.E.T. Omnibus Services Ltd and Tilling Motor Services Ltd. The former was to be controlled by the British Electric Traction Co Ltd, and the latter by Thomas Tilling

Ltd. Southdown returned to the B.E.T. fold, its original home. R P Beddow, Secretary of B.E.T., joined Southdown in place of Tilling's Thomas Wolsey. This move also brought about the end of the close links between Southdown and Wilts & Dorset, the latter company finding itself in the Tilling camp and therefore required to adopt standard Tilling Group livery and purchase only vehicles of Bristol/ECW manufacture.

While the completion of 'unfrozen' buses and the increase in the capacity of single-deckers went some way towards easing the situation, it was but a drop in the ocean. The Ministry of Supply, the Ministry of War Transport, operators and manufacturers therefore set about drawing up specifications for a bus that would be serviceable but at a minimum cost in terms of materials and skilled labour. The result was what we now know as the 'utility' double-decker. (There was also a single-deck version, which need not concern us as none were supplied to Southdown.) Supplies of aluminium were being directed to the aircraft industry so metal was used in

A number of livery styles were applied in an effort to make buses less conspicuous from the air. Initially single-deckers were given dark green roofs, something that was perpetuated after the end of the war. Many double-deckers were similarly treated but, as the war progressed, various combinations of grey, green and sometimes cream were applied. It is not always easy to discern from a black and white photograph exactly what the colours were, but 157 (EUF 157), a Leyland TD5 with lowbridge Park Royal bodywork appears to be in apple green with cream lower deck window surrounds, coincidentally the livery chosen for double-deckers by the privatised Southdown in 1986. Haywards Heath is the location. *(W J Haynes/Southdown Enthusiasts' Club)*

its place. Body framing was of timber, often unseasoned, which led to problems in later life. The body itself was designed with the absolute minimum of curved panels, thus obviating the need for skilled panel beaters. The specification itself was basic, to say the least. Only one opening window per side was allowed on each deck, although ventilators were to be provided on the front upper deck windows. Initially the rear upper deck window was to be panelled over in sheet metal, although this was later relaxed. Wooden slatted seats were fitted to the early examples.

Whilst this was the design laid down by the MoS, bodybuilders used their own interpretation of the specification, resulting in considerable variations in the degree of austerity,

Rather surprisingly, Guy Motors Ltd, which had not hitherto been in the forefront of bus manufacture, was initially chosen as the chassis-builder for double-deckers, although it was later joined by Bristol and Daimler. Unlike many operators, including neighbouring Maidstone & District which had a mixture of chassis makes, the one hundred utilities supplied to Southdown were all of Guy manufacture. The Arab II, as the Guy chassis was named, could be supplied with either the Gardner 5LW or 6LW engines, whilst the body could be of either highbridge or lowbridge layout.

Southdown came through the war with remarkably little damage to vehicles and buildings. One casualty was Harrington-bodied Leyland TS8 1443 (FCD 243). Originally similar to the bus on the title page, it was badly damaged in an air attack at Punnetts Town, near Heathfield on 2nd November 1940. It was blown down an embankment, killing five passengers and the conductor. The body was scrapped but the chassis was repaired and fitted with a pre-war Metcalfe 32-seat coach body, which Harrington happened to have. It was most un-Southdown like with its centre entrance, stepped waistline and no canopy over the nearside of the driver's cab. In this form it ran until 1952 when the body was removed and the chassis used to provide components for Beadle rebuild 876 (MCD 876). (*Roy Marshall/Southdown Enthusiasts' Club*)

The first examples for Southdown arrived in 1943, the last being delivered in March 1946. Quite remarkably all but a handful had matching fleet and registration numbers, something that was virtually unheard of during the war years. This would have pleased Alfred Douglas Mackenzie and it is probably appropriate here to record that the Guys were the last new Southdown vehicles that he saw, as he died in 1944 at the age of 74.

Utilities on Parade

The Northern Counties body was the most numerous amongst Southdown's utilities, starting the Company's long association with the Lancashire coachbuilder. Unlike those of the other three manufacturers, NCME's bodies were metal framed, making them far more durable than their composite counterparts. The bodies were also the least angular with deep roofs and gently curved front and rear domes. Northern Counties-bodied 417 (GUF 117) crosses Broadwater Bridge in Worthing. Note the traditional British 'Bobby' cycling in the opposite direction. *(Southdown Enthusiasts' Club)*

485 (GUF 185) was one of the last utilities for Southdown, being delivered in September 1945, and illustrates Weymann's interpretation of the austerity body. One or two, including this one, had what appears to be Weymann's standard pre-war cab door, definitely not part of the Ministry of Supply's specification. Southdown's wartime Arabs were delivered with a mixture of five and six cylinder Gardner engines, the 6-cylinder version originally being identifiable by the protruding bonnet. However engines were interchanged during their lifetimes, some losing 5LW engines in favour of the six cylinder version and vice-versa. 485 was converted to open top in 1958 and its body was then transferred to an earlier Arab, 412. *(W J Haynes/ Southdown Enthusiasts' Club)*

Renew and Repair – Post War Recovery

The war in Europe came to an end on 8th May 1945, but there was no overnight end to hardship. Rationing continued; there were still shortages and long queues for necessities. The main difference was that these difficulties were faced with optimism in the belief that there was a better world to come. Petrol was still in short supply; in fact it was to be another five years before petrol rationing ended. But despite the difficulties, or maybe because of them, the British people were intent on enjoying themselves and, as soon as the barbed wire and mines were removed, the trippers returned to the seaside *en masse.*

Unfortunately the coach fleet was sadly depleted, due largely to the number of coaches that had been requisitioned by the military, many never to return, and those that remained had been out of use for six years and were badly in need of attention. The bus fleet was still pretty well intact but many of the vehicles were well past their normal 'sell-by' date. Renewal of the fleet was therefore important but, with most of the country's operators in the same position, new vehicles were in great demand and delivery times were slow. As an interim measure Southdown looked to the rebuilding and re-bodying programme, which was instigated in 1945 and continued through to 1950.

However, the first operational development began in May 1945 when talks started between Southdown and Portsmouth Corporation with a view to co-ordinating services. Portsmouth had suffered severely from German bombing raids; it was obvious that there would be a need for new housing and that much of it would

The first post-war double-deckers were 25 Leyland PD1s with Park Royal 54-seat bodies. As can be seen the body style was little different from the utility design fitted to the wartime Guys but with the addition of some characteristic Southdown features originating from pre-war buses. They included the metal sun visor above the windscreen and a small curved staircase window on the offside of the lower deck. 266 (GUF 666) is seen as delivered, with dark green roof and green-painted radiator. On the right is Northern Counties-bodied Guy Arab 465 (GUF 165) delivered in 1945 and showing just how similar to the utility design was the Park Royal body on the PD1. Judging from the crowds in Pool Valley, life was rapidly returning to normal. *(Omnibus Society)*

A typical rural Sussex scene with Park Royal-bodied Leyland PD1 271 (GUF 671) at Pevensey Bay heading for Eastbourne on local route 96. *(G H F Atkins)*

With their 7.4 litre engines, the PD1s proved to be vastly underpowered and most graduated to the relatively flat terrain of the Worthing area. Worthing sea front west of the Pier is the location for this fine shot of 287 (GUF 687). *(Chris Nash/P M Photography)*

The Park Royal PD1 was immortalised by appearing on the cover of the Southdown timetable for very many years. First introduced on the 1946 timetable, the cover was impressionistic and, for Southdown, unusually colourful. The PD1 was shown with dark green roof climbing an exaggeratedly steep hill, which its 7.4 litre engine could never have managed!

By 1949 the design had become much more sober. The PD1 now had a cream roof and could be identified as car 280 (GUF 680). The location appeared to be Sanatorium Hill leading out of Eastbourne. *(Glyn Kraemer-Johnson Collection)*

probably be built away from the City centre. It was therefore in the interests of the Corporation that it should benefit from any such expansion, while passengers would gain by being able to travel to the more outlying areas without having to change buses as was the case then. It was agreed that services operated within an area bounded by Fareham, Petersfield and Emsworth should be co-ordinated and that the revenue and mileage should be pooled on a percentage basis, 57% to the Corporation and 43% to Southdown. The Joint Services Agreement came into effect on 1st July 1946 and was to last for 21 years.

The need for new vehicles and, in particular new and rebuilt bodies, was obviously not confined to Southdown but was duplicated by almost every bus and coach operator in the country. Needless to say the established manufacturers were unable to meet the demand and this resulted in a number of newcomers to the fold. A number of coach builders that before the war had been engaged in building coachwork for luxury cars, for which there was now little or no demand, turned their attention to the construction of passenger vehicles.

Similarly several concerns which had been involved in aircraft production now found themselves with empty order books and saw an opportunity to compensate by turning their attention to

the passenger transport industry. Thus in the late forties and early fifties a number of unfamiliar names appeared amongst the ranks of bus and coach manufacturers.

Southdown's 1400-class TS7 and TS8 single-deckers were amongst the first to be dealt with. Between 1945 and 1949 those which had been converted to perimeter seating were restored to their original B32R layout and most had their bodies rebuilt by a number of concerns including Portsmouth Aviation, Lancashire Aircraft, Aircraft Dispatch, the local motor dealer Caffyns and Southdown itself.

The first new double-deckers were delivered in the spring and summer of 1946 and were of Leyland's post war PD1 type with Park Royal bodies. The chassis was fitted with Leyland's new E181 engine of 7.4 litres that had been developed during the war for use in military vehicles and proved to be vastly underpowered for bus use.

The return of the day-trippers saw the 1929 TD1s have their wartime top covers removed and, after a repaint, being put to work on seasonal services, such as that to Devil's Dyke.

1947 proved to be an eventful year in many ways. In June, joint founder of the Company, Alfred Cannon, retired as General Manager, his place being taken by A F R Carling who had managed

In 1948 Southdown took delivery of no fewer than 80 of Leyland's newly-introduced PD2, all of which carried Leyland's own 54-seat bodywork. Seen when new, still with full lining-out and dark green radiator surround, 336 (JCD 36) stands in Pool Valley, Brighton before setting off on the long journey to Southsea. *(C Carter)*

Sister bus 334 (JCD 34) pauses at Hassocks Station in September 1962, having arrived on the local service from Hurstpierpoint. *(Southdown Enthusiasts' Club)*

Obviously impressed by the rugged reliability of its Northern Counties-bodied Guy utilities, something of a stir was caused when a further twelve vehicles of the same chassis/body combination were delivered in 1948/49. These were Arab IIIs with Gardner 6LW engines and the Northern Counties bodies were very much to peacetime standards. With Guy's low bonnet line, which enabled horizontal lower edges to the bulkhead and driver's windows, they were particularly handsome buses. The twelve were divided between Brighton and Portsmouth and were rarely, if ever seen elsewhere. 506 (JCD 506) was one of Portsmouth's allocation and is seen here at Northern Road, Cosham when new, looking resplendent in fully lined-out livery.
(Surfleet/Southdown Enthusiasts' Club)

the hard hit Portsmouth Area throughout the war. Cannon retained his seat on the board until his death in 1952. It was also the year in which Britain's railways were nationalised and the Southern Railway's one third share in Southdown therefore became owned by the Government. This had no visible effect on Southdown's operations or the appearance of its vehicles, unlike the Tilling Group companies, which passed into State ownership at the same time and which were obliged to standardise on vehicle types and, in most cases to adopt a corporate livery style.

The year also saw a much-needed influx of new vehicles. For stage carriage work came a further twenty-five Leyland PD1 double-deckers, but this time they had Leyland's own bodywork. Basically an updated version of its pre-war design, which itself had been based on the London trolleybus bodies built by Leyland in the thirties, they were nonetheless very handsome vehicles. Unfortunately they still had the inadequate 7.4 litre E181 engine and thus proved as sluggish and underpowered as their Park Royal-bodied counterparts.

In 1947 Leyland introduced its Titan PD2 chassis, which featured the larger 0.600 engine of 9.8 litres capacity and was a vast improvement over its 7.4 litre predecessor. In fact the 0.600 became something of an icon, remaining in production until 1972. It provided the power for Southdown's Leyland double-deckers until the last front-engined chassis was received in 1967. In 1948 Southdown received no fewer than 80 Leyland PD2/1s, numbered 316-395 (JCD 16-95), all of which were fitted with Leyland's own all-metal bodies seating 54, and being very similar to those received on PD1 chassis. These handsome buses were put to work on the Company's front line services.

A further twelve double-deckers arrived in 1949, causing some surprise for they were Guy Arab IIIs with Gardner 6LW engines and Northern Counties bodies, Southdown obviously having been impressed by the rugged reliability by the wartime double-deckers of the same chassis/body combination. They were much different in appearance, however, Northern Counties having returned to its typical rounded Lancastrian style with heavily radiused corners to

One of the twelve Guys differed from the rest of the batch. 502 (JCD 502) had been exhibited on the Northern Counties stand at the 1948 Commercial Motor Show and was fitted with the bodybuilder's patent heating and ventilation system. The body design itself was again considerably different to the other eleven. The front and rear upper deck windows were heavily radiused as were the front and rear side windows. On the lower deck, small 'standee' windows were fitted above the main side windows and a finishing touch was the chrome surround to the front destination box. The bus was not unique, similar vehicles being supplied to Lancashire United and Western SMT, but there was never any problem distinguishing it from the rest of the Southdown fleet. 502 is seen in Pool Valley, Brighton in September 1953 waiting to depart on service 20 to Chailey. *(Michael Dryhurst)*

the front and rear windows. The twelve Guys were divided between Brighton and Portsmouth where they remained throughout their working lives.

1949 also saw the delivery of the Company's last half-cab single-deckers, these again being a little unusual. Numbered 82-91 (JUF 82-91), they were Dennis Falcons with 30-seat bodies also by Dennis and were purchased especially for the Hayling Island services on which they spent their entire lives. As well as being the last front-engined saloons, they were also the first single-deckers purchased since the war. Having built up a fleet of more than eighty Harrington-bodied Leyland Tigers during the 1930s, these stalwarts, together with the versatile little Cubs, maintained Southdown's single-deck services until replaced by underfloor-engined saloons and, even then many soldiered on well into the mid-fifties.

Express services were reintroduced in March 1946, but not before the coaches, many of which had lain idle for six years, had been cleaned, repainted where necessary, had any damage repaired

and had their 'Southdown Sparkle' restored. The coach fleet was sadly depleted due to the requisitions by the Military but, with most operators throughout the country being in a similar position, new vehicles were not immediately available, coachbuilders being particularly hard-pressed. Southdown placed orders for 125 Leyland PS1 chassis, this being the equivalent of the PD1 double-decker with the same E181 engine of 7.4 litre capacity. As with the rebodied TDs, bodywork was shared between six coachbuilders, some of which were new to Southdown.

The first to arrive were 25 with 'Express' bodies by Eastern Coachworks, a company normally associated with the Tilling Group operators, The 'Express' single-deck design was what today we would call 'dual-purpose'; a standard bus shell fitted with coach seats. Bus-like they may have been, indeed many of them were modified for bus work later in their lives, but they were very attractive vehicles and looked particularly well in Southdown livery. They were put to work on London to South Coast express services, bringing some relief to the over-worked pre-war coach fleet.

New Bodies for Old

Unlike many operators which set about rebodying wartime chassis, Southdown embarked on an extensive programme of fitting new bodies to no fewer than 153 of its pre-war Leyland Titan TD3s, 4s and 5s. The work was carried out by five manufacturers, Beadle, East Lancs, Northern Counties, Park Royal and, a new name for Southdown, Saunders Engineering. The following photographs illustrate the very different ways in which these body-builders tackled the task.

Looking almost more old-fashioned than the Park Royal body it replaced is the six-bay body by J C Beadle of Dartford, which was fitted to Leyland TD5 153 (DUF 153) in July 1948. The six-bay layout had been popular during the thirties but by the outbreak of war had largely been replaced by five, and in some cases even four bays. Beadle, however, stuck doggedly to its six-bays. Despite its somewhat antiquated design, the bus looked particularly smart in its fully lined-out livery and with precisely-set destination blinds when photographed at Southsea prior to departing for Waterlooville. *(Omnibus Society)*

By 1949, when this TD4 received its new body, Beadle had relented and was building bodies to the more popular five-bay layout. Southdown therefore had a mixture of both types. 141 (CCD 941) was already thirteen years old when its original Beadle lowbridge body was replaced and it went on to serve the company for a further ten years. It is seen waiting in the wings at the entrance to Worthing depot before setting off on the historic service 1 to Pulborough. *(W J Haynes/Southdown Enthusiasts' Club)*

This offside view of sister bus 168 (EUF 168) shows the gently curving frontal profile and generally 'un-utility' like appearance of the East Lancs body. In fact it bore more than a passing resemblance to the post-war Leyland body. It was photographed in Worthing nearing the end of its life but still with lined-out livery. *(Cliff Essex)*

By June 1949 when 213 received its new body, East Lancs had updated its design to incorporate the radiused corners to the front upper deck windows that were to give East Lancs bodies their characteristic appearance for several years. The location is Brighton's Pool Valley bus station, always a Mecca for the enthusiast and an ideal spot for the photographer as evidenced by this picture. Southdown 213 (FCD 513), was a TD5 dating from 1939 that had originally carried a lowbridge body by Park Royal. The photograph would appear to have been taken shortly after the new body was fitted judging by the full lining-out, the absence of adverts and the generally sparkling appearance – although the latter was not confined to new or newly painted vehicles. *(W J Haynes/Southdown Enthusiasts' Club)*

In the days when cigarette advertising provided a good deal of revenue for bus operators, sister bus 212 (FCD 512) is seen a little later in its life. The lining out at roof level has gone, but remains elsewhere. Like 213 it too carried a lowbridge Park Royal body when new. It was photographed at Cowfold, waiting to depart for Haywards Heath. *(Alan Cross)*

223 (FUF 223) was a Leyland TD5 dating from 1939. It received this new Park Royal body in May 1949 and, although having lost its dark green lining out, still looked in fine fettle when photographed. *(Southdown Enthusiasts' Club)*

The overall appearance of the Saunders body was not dissimilar to that of Park Royal's. Apart from the staircase window, just discernible in this view, the most obvious difference was the curved beading beneath the windscreen. 115 (BUF 215) was a TD4 new in 1934. It had previously carried a lowbridge body by Short Bros. When new it had been classified TD4c indicating that it was fitted with a torque convertor, this being removed in 1946/7. It was photographed at Worthing Garage. *(Cliff Essex)*

154 (DUF 154) was one of just four TD5s delivered in 1937. Originally fitted with a Park Royal body, it received this Northern Counties one in February 1950. The pre-war TDs were regular performers on Brighton local services and 154 is seen coasting towards the Old Steine terminus but with blinds already set for the return journey. *(John Kaye)*

The remaining PS1s had 'pure' coach bodies, the coachwork being split between Beadle, Harrington and Park Royal whose products were already to be found in the fleet and the two newcomers, Duple and Windover. Delivered throughout 1948 and 1949, they were used on various duties including excursions, private hire and some express work. Two more coaches arrived in 1948, which proved to be the Company's last new front-engined coaches – well, almost. They were also to remain unique in the fleet being petrol-engined Bedford OBs with virtually standard Duple bodies, although in true Southdown tradition the seating was reduced to 27 instead of the usual 29. The reason for this unusual purchase was 'that darned bridge', the Langstone Bridge between Hayling Island and the mainland with its severe weight restrictions, the OBs being put to work on the Hayling Island to London express service.

The immediate post-war years saw something of a boom in express services, mainly due to servicemen travelling to and from home on leave and this continued into the fifties with those called up for National Service. The fact that many of these servicemen were travelling long distances to and from their camps, led to the operation of joint services giving direct connections with destinations far out of the Southdown area.

In conjunction with Channel Airways, the company launched a coach-air service to the Channel Islands that lasted into the National Bus Company era.

Re-introduced in 1945 using a motley collection of vehicles, excursions, too, were proving immensely popular. Released from wartime restrictions, the public was determined to make the most of its freedom and to enjoy its leisure time. Hence, as soon as the barricades had been removed, the trippers returned in their droves. In fact Southdown's 1946 Excursion programme was larger than those it had operated prior to the outbreak of hostilities.

Coach Cruises were a little later in returning, being reintroduced in 1947, although this was due largely to the difficulty in finding hotel accommodation, rather than through any fault of the Company. The new coaches delivered in the late forties did not include any tourers, so the Lionesses soldiered on until the early fifties when they were replaced by new underfloor-engined coaches.

Park Royal was a regular provider of bodywork for Southdown, both double-deckers and coaches being supplied during the 1930s and later building utility bodies on Guy Arab chassis during the war. The association continued in peacetime and following on from the PD1 double-deckers came 25 Leyland PS1s with Park Royal 32-seat coach bodies that were used mainly on excursion and private hire work, but occasionally ventured onto express services. Whilst the ECW-bodied PS1s handled most of the London services, they were rarely seen on the South Coast Express, this usually being worked by vehicles to full coach specification. When reintroduced after the war, the South Coast Express was jointly operated by Southdown and East Kent, running from Margate to Portsmouth where it connected with Royal Blue services to Bournemouth and the West of England. Here we see Park Royal-bodied Leyland PS1 1256 (HCD 856) pausing at Bexhill on its way to Folkestone. Interestingly the Park Royal bodies for Southdown were based on a specification by East Kent for its own Leyland PS1s, one of which (CFN 90) is seen behind apparently running *in tandem* with the Southdown coach. *(Omnibus Society)*

'Streamlined' was a word very much in vogue during the late thirties. It referred to aerodynamic and often bulbous designs that were applied, amongst other things, to motor cars, railway locomotives and to a number of coaches. Thomas Harrington of Hove turned away from its usual restrained designs and introduced a flamboyant and futuristic body which, as well as its excessively curvaceous body featured what became known as the 'dorsal fin'. This was a triangular casing fitted between the rear windows that housed a patent ventilation system. Although one of the most prolific builders of Southdown coaches, Harrington's bodied just 6 Leyland PS1s, 1264-9 (HUF 4-9). After the war the design was refined to become a very attractive half-cab coach but the dorsal fin remained. Southdown, always conservative in its taste, declined such embellishments and on all but one of these coaches specified also a full-width canopy that seemed to give the vehicles a much more business-like appearance. The company did, however, allow three decorative strips to be applied behind the rear wheel! Waiting on Brighton sea front to take up an excursion duty, 1269 (HUF 9) shows off its gleaming paintwork, the effect being only marginally spoilt by the painted radiator which these coaches carried when new. (W J Haynes/Southdown Enthusiasts' Club)

By the summer of 1948 the excursion programme was back in full swing, with day and half-day trips to local beauty spots and places of interest, as well as the ever-popular trips to sporting events such as Royal Ascot and local race meetings at Brighton, Lewes, Fontwell, Plumpton and, of course, the ever-popular 'Glorious Goodwood'. (Author's Collection)

Windover was a name new to Southdown; in fact it was a name new to motor-coach bodybuilding. However, it was a company with a long and interesting history, dating back to the early 17th century when it was established as a saddle maker. It had progressed through carriage-building to producing high-quality bodywork for luxury cars such as Rolls-Royce, Daimler and Bentley. During and after the Second World War the demand for sumptuous limousines vanished and Windover, along with other builders of quality coachwork, saw a niche in the market for the construction of bodywork for motor coaches. It produced a half-cab luxury coach body named the 'Huntingdon' after the location of its factory. Southdown took just six of these bodies on Leyland PS1 chassis numbered 1270-1275 (HUF 270-5), which were delivered in the late autumn of 1947. Whilst similar to other coaches of the period, the Windover body was sleek, elegant and decidedly handsome. It had no canopy, although the roof did protrude slightly over the nearside front window. The upper part of the windscreen was angled backwards, leading into the swept-back line of the front dome, and the waistline curved downwards towards the rear. The most distinguishing feature was the pear-shaped mouldings around the wheel-arches, which quickly became known as 'tear drops'. Their elegant lines fitted well into Southdown's style. *(From a painting by John Kinsley/Transport Art)*

1238 (GUF 738) was the first of the ECW-bodied PS1s to arrive, being delivered in February 1947. This official photograph taken one month before, shows the coach to have standard ECW sliding vents, together with cream cant panels and a larger area of cream around the destination screen than was subsequently used. *(Eastern Coachworks/ S J Butler archive)*

Southdown appeared to have had an inherent dislike of sliding ventilators, finally adopting them long after most other operators outside London. Presumably this was the reason for various experimental window designs being fitted to some of the ECW PS1s when new. 1244 (GUF 744) was also delivered in February 1947 but this photograph, also by the body-builder is dated September 1947, suggesting that the vehicle may have been returned for modification. As can be seen, it carries the standard livery worn by these coaches, but is fitted with three-quarter depth sliding windows of almost tropical style. *(Eastern Coachworks/S J Butler Archive)*

The third photo shows 1246 outside the ECW factory and is dated February 1948, although the vehicle was delivered to Southdown in March 1947. This one is fitted with full-depth sliding windows; not particularly suited to the British climate, one would have thought! *(Eastern Coachworks/S J Butler Archive)*

The Company finally settled on its much favoured half-drop windows as illustrated by 1227 (GUF 727), seen early in its life, still with painted radiator. Later modified for bus work, this vehicle is fortunately still with us in preservation. *(Alan Lambert/Southdown Enthusiasts' Club)*

It was a pity that a fleet of 125 coaches of between two and four years old should become obsolete overnight, but that is what happened when, in 1951, the first underfloor-engined coaches arrived. The traditional radiator had disappeared, as it had on many private cars and the half-cab had also gone, both replaced by a modernistic full front with decorative mouldings and a small grille. Despite their young age, the PSIs now looked antiquated and no longer what the public expected and so, along with many other operators, Southdown set about modernising at least some of them. The Beadle and Duple examples were sent off to Beadle in 1954-55 for rebuilding with full fronts. The design used was basically that of the integral rebuilds then being produced by the Dartford company at that time and, whether they originally had Beadle or Duple bodies, the rebuilt coaches were virtually indistinguishable. Full-front conversions were rarely successful and these were no exception, having lost much of the elegance of the original bodywork. However, they may have convinced some of the travelling public that they were more modern than was really the case! 1350 (HUF 950) originally carried a Duple body and was, in fact, the penultimate PSI to be delivered, arriving in November 1949. It was photographed at Victoria Coach Station in company with another of its kind. *(P M Photography)*

The Beadle-bodied PSI is illustrated by 1288 (HUF 288) seen working to Oxford on hire to South Midland Motor Services. *(Author's Collection)*

A Bridge Too Weak

The majority of Southdown's Leyland Cubs were of normal control layout, the bus version usually seating 20. However, in 1936/7 the Company took delivery of six SKPZ2 forward control models with Park Royal 26-seat bodies, the forward control layout enabling an extra six seats to be accommodated. All six were allocated to the Hayling Island service and spent their entire working lives in the Havant area. All were withdrawn in 1956 following the opening of the new bridge. Pictured here is car number 8 (DUF 8), delivered in January 1937, looking extremely smart and with neatly lined-up destination screen. Note the roof luggage rack. *(Surfleet/Southdown Enthusiasts' Club)*

To operate the express service from Hayling to London and excursions to and from the Island, Southdown chose a type new to the fleet, the Leyland Cheetah. Eleven of these coaches were delivered, five in 1938 and a further six the following year. They were fitted with 24-seat centre-entrance bodies by Park Royal. Like the Cubs they remained in the Hayling area throughout their lives and were withdrawn on the opening of the new bridge. Seen on the London Express service is 505 (FUF 505) of the second batch. *(Author's Collection)*

Although Southdown only operated two Bedford OBs, they have been immortalised by a number of model manufacturers in at least four different scales, such is the attraction of the Southdown name and livery. Number 70 is illustrated in this painting by John Kinsey. *(From a painting by John Kinsley/Transport Art Collections)*

The Years of Plenty

The 1950s were golden years for bus operators in a number of respects. At the beginning of the decade car ownership was still low – indeed, fuel rationing was still in place – and for the normal working man and his family the bus was the normal form of transport whether it be to work, school, shopping or for pleasure. The cinema still thrived and many families would 'go to the pictures' at least once, possibly twice a week. Foreign holidays had yet to be within reach of the majority and for most families it was still usual for their two weeks' annual holiday to be spent at the seaside. Thus the buses and excursion coaches were kept busy and the operators happy.

As well as the rejuvenation and renewal of its bus and coach fleet, Southdown also embarked on a fairly extensive building programme. A much-needed bus station and garage were built at Chichester, removing the buses from the congested area around the cathedral. Two more were built at Haywards Heath and Lewes, while Crawley and Seaford received new garages. Other buildings were extended including the Central Works at Portslade.

Acquisitions continued to a lesser degree including, in the west, Triumph Coaches of Portsmouth purchased in May 1957 (of which more later) and, in October 1959, P. W. Lambert (trading as Little Wonder Coaches) which operated a service from Petersfield to Buriton. Beacon Motor Services of Crowborough was fully absorbed into the Company in 1954 (although it had been controlled by Southdown since 1949. H J Sargent of East Grinstead was taken into the fold in March 1951. This company, which traded as East Grinstead Coaches, operated three stage carriage services; East Grinstead to Crowborough, East Grinstead to Ashurst Wood and East Grinstead to Cowden. Following these last two acquisitions there was a reorganisation of services in the area with some passing to neighbouring Maidstone & District. A further reorganisation took place in 1958, this time in Crawley, one of the 'New Towns' built to take the overspill from London. Again there was a reallocation of services, this time between Southdown and London Transport.

There had long been joint working between Southdown and M&D on services between Eastbourne and Hastings, Brighton and Hawkhurst, Brighton and Tunbridge Wells and, from 1948,

Chichester Garage opened in 1956, and this view shows its proximity to the railway line. In view are two Leyland Royal Tiger coaches and an East Lancs-bodied PD2 in the garage, while a Maidstone & District coach lurks behind the foliage. In the foreground, a Northern Counties-bodied PD3 is on the stand in the bus station opposite. *(Southdown Enthusiasts' Club)*

The bus station at Chichester, situated on the opposite side of the service road, was the largest of three built by Southdown in the 1950s, the other two being at Lewes and Haywards Heath. At the time of writing (2014) the complex remains in use by Stagecoach. Note the Leyland Tiger Cub saloon on the left, still with dark green roof. *(Southdown Enthusiasts' Club)*

Another imposing frontage was that of Haywards Heath Bus Station in Perrymount Road, again next to the Railway Station. It was photographed on a wintry day two months or so before its opening in May 1956. *(Southdown Chronicle/Stagecoach South)*

Haywards Heath – fully operational with a Leyland Royal Tiger saloon in the foreground, a Leyland PD2/I behind and an attractive floral display to the right. Sadly this fine building has now been demolished. *(Southdown Enthusiasts' Club)*

The third of the new bus stations was located at Lewes. Built on similar lines to that at Haywards Heath, it differed in having a garage within its boundaries. It still exists at the time of writing but, with the garage and offices no longer in use, it is little more than a bus terminal and waiting room – although the café remains open. *(Southdown Enthusiasts' Club)*

The Seaford garage built in 1957 was Southdown's third garage in the town. *(Southdown Enthusiasts' Club)*

Crawley Garage was built as a result of expansion due to the building of Crawley New Town and adjoined the County Oak coach station. In this 1962 view, a Beadle-bodied Leyland Tiger Cub stands at the entrance beside an unusually deserted coach station. *(Southdown Enthusiasts' Club)*

The garage at Moulsecoomb, on the outskirts of Brighton was opened in 1958 to provide extra capacity and to relieve overcrowding at the town's other garages, particularly those at Park Street and The Vicarage. Ever longer vehicles take up more space! Two all-Leyland PD2/1s stand in the roadway outside. *(Southdown Enthusiasts' Club)*

Brighton and Gravesend. However, 1957 saw the introduction of what was known as the 'Heathfield Pool' or 'Heathfield Cycle'. Under this arrangement six services from Brighton, Eastbourne, Hastings, Hawkhurst and Tunbridge Wells were timed to connect at Heathfield, a small market town on the ridge of the Sussex Weald. This arrangement provided passengers with a much improved service and, through fairer pooling of receipts, actually allowed for a reduction in fares. The arrangement, which was a masterly example of time-tabling and co-ordination, lasted until April 1971 when falling traffic made it no longer viable.

The 1950s saw a number of changes of senior personnel. A F R Carling was appointed to an executive position with B.E.T. and his place with Southdown was taken by Arthur Woodgate. In the 1930s Mr Woodgate had been Assistant Chief Engineer with East Midland, later becoming Chief Engineer within that company. He moved to North Western Road Car in the same capacity. He later took up the post of Chief Engineer with Ribble Motor Services, subsequently becoming Assistant General Manager before moving to Southdown as General Manager.

1958 saw the retirement of Chief Engineer Mr H R Lane after twenty-eight years with the company, his place being taken by Mr W G Hall. Hall, who had been educated at St George's School, Edgbaston and the Birmingham Technical School, had decided on transport as a career at the end of the 1914-1918 war and joined the Birmingham & Midland Motor Omnibus Co. Ltd (Midland Red)

in 1920. He had started with that Company as Assistant Garage Foreman, was appointed Technical Foreman in 1927 and five years later became Engineering Superintendent. In 1941 he was appointed Area Engineer in charge of the Southern Area of the Company and in 1947 was promoted to Rolling Stock Engineer for the whole of the Company's outside garages. He became Chief Engineer of the Potteries Motor Traction Co. Ltd in June 1952, moving to Southdown in 1958.

Appointed in 1958, Mr W G Hall took over from Mr Lane as Chief Engineer. *(Southdown Chronicle/ Stagecoach South)*

'Unlucky 700'

Southdown's unique double-deck coach 700 (KUF 700) poses for admiration at Victoria Coach Station, following its appearance at the 1950 Commercial Motor Show. There was little doubt that the origins of the Northern Counties 44-seat body could be traced back to 502, the experimental Guy Arab of 1948. However, this body was of four-bay construction and interestingly was the only double-decker bought new by Southdown to be of this layout. Another first for a Southdown double-decker was the enclosed rear platform equipped with electrically operated jack-knife doors. Internally the coach was fitted with full-height luggage racks in the lower saloon over the rear wheels while Perspex 'quarter-lights' in the roof allowed additional light to the upper deck. Seating was to full coach specification incorporating head-rests. The most striking feature was probably the full-front with enclosed radiator, the design of which was clearly a precursor of the iconic 'Queen Mary' Leyland PD3s. *(Omnibus Society)*

Proving to be over the legal weight limit when fitted with 58 bus seats, 700 was given 50 coach seats and used on private hire and short excursions from Bognor, proving quite successful with holidaymakers on short trips to Southsea and with the company because of its high revenue per mile in this role. It is seen here enjoying a final fling on a Southdown Enthusiasts' Club tour in September 1962. *(Southdown Enthusiasts' Club)*

1951 was the year of the Festival of Britain, a shop window to show the world Britain's achievements in industry, design and culture, as well as to boost the morale of the British people following the dismal years of shortages and deprivation brought about by the Second World War. Southdown was represented by the first of its all-Leyland PD2/12s, 701 (KUF 701) being displayed at the Festival. *(London Transport Museum)*

Where to go by Southdown leaflet featuring an all-Leyland PD2/12. *(Paul Gainsbury Collection)*

Seen in September 1963, by which time it had received the simplified livery minus lining out, 726 (LUF 226), from the second batch of PD2/12s, crosses the boundary between Hove and Portslade en *route* for Littlehampton. Under the BATS Agreement, service 9 was diverted away from the sea front to operate via Brighton Station and Old Shoreham Road, previously the preserve of Brighton Hove & District. *(Southdown Enthusiasts' Club)*

1950 was something of a milestone for bus and coach operators across the UK. July saw the maximum permitted dimensions for PSVS increased. The maximum width was increased from 7ft 6in to 8ft and four-wheel double-deckers could now be 27ft long. The maximum length for coaches and single-deckers was increased to 30ft. This obviously allowed for increased seating capacity, that of double-deckers commonly being between 60 and 65. Southdown increased the capacity of its double-deckers from a modest 54 to an equally modest 58.

The same year also saw the introduction on a large scale of the underfloor-engined single-decker. Experimental single-deckers had been built to this layout since before the war but, in 1950 all the major manufacturers introduced underfloor-engined chassis. With the engine tucked away beneath the floor, there was more space for seating and, particularly important for coach work, the driver was no longer isolated in his separate cab, but seated in the main body of the vehicle. The downside was that half-cab single-deckers and particularly coaches, some of which were only a year or two old, became virtually obsolete overnight. There were various attempts to update them, some more successful than others, but it soon became clear that the chassis with its engine amidships was here to stay.

It was common practice for Southdown to replace the chassis manufacturers' nameplates with its own, which somehow seemed a little unfair, especially on underfloor-engined chassis on which the name on the wheel hubs often became the only means of identification: even more so when the badges replaced were as attractive as the Leyland Royal Tiger and Tiger Cub emblems. Seen here is Southdown's replacement. *(Glyn Kraemer-Johnson/Ian Richardson Collection)*

1511 basks in the sunshine on Worthing sea front. This was one of the second batch of East Lancs-bodied Leyland Royal Tigers, numbered 1510-38 with corresponding MCD registrations, which had central rather than rear entrances. By the time this photograph was taken 1511 had been converted to front entrance to enable one man operation, as indeed were all of the type. *(Martin Jenkins)*

Twenty Tiger Cub saloons were delivered in 1954 with bodies by Nudd Bros & Lockyer. These were followed in 1955 by a further four, this time with bodies by Park Royal, outwardly similar to the Nudd Bros examples, but there were differences, notably the window arrangement with one fewer window per side. The windscreens, too, were deeper, but the most noticeable change was the waist rail, the downward curve of which was convex rather than concave as on the Nudd Bros and East Lancs saloons. These features are well-illustrated in these official bodybuilder's photographs of 641 (OUF 641), which show just how attractive these buses were – and how very much Southdown. *(Park Royal Vehicles/Glyn Kraemer-Johnson Collection)*

1955 saw the arrival of a further twelve Leyland PD2/12s (top) and twelve Guy Arab IVs (below), all of which had 59-seat bodies by Park Royal. This official body-builder's photograph shows the classic lines of the Park Royal body of that time which, hardly surprisingly, bore a strong resemblance to the London RT, of which Park Royal had bodied the majority. However, whilst most Park Royal bodies of the time were of four bay construction, Southdown doggedly continued to specify five. *(Graham Hill collection)*

During the mid to late 1950s many operators were specifying lightweight bodies, devoid of any unnecessary fittings, sometimes cramming as many as 65 passengers into a 27ft double-decker. Not so Southdown. It maintained a capacity of 59 well-spaced seats after the initial increase to 58. Seat backs were shaped to give maximum comfort whilst the traditional brown and cream interior panels were trimmed with varnished wood. As can be seen from this official picture of a Park Royal-bodied Guy Arab, the whole combined to give an air of subdued elegance and comfort. Few stage carriage vehicles of the time could boast such luxurious interiors. *(Park Royal Vehicles/ Author's Collection)*

The long service 122 from Brighton to Gravesend was usually the preserve of Leyland PD2s but Guys were also used, as on this occasion in 1968 when 532 (PUF 632) was photographed at Borough Green. The front bulkhead on the Park Royal body was possibly designed for the 'tin-fronted' AEC Regent V. On the PD2 the window was unnecessarily high and on the Guy, with its low bonnet line, even more so. However, this was a minor point and did little to detract from the vehicle's extremely handsome appearance. Unfortunately, in the decade that followed Park Royal would produce some of the ugliest double-deckers to be built. *(Southdown Enthusiasts' Club Collection)*

Southdown's choice of double-deck chassis to the new dimensions was unsurprisingly the Leyland PD2/12 and, apart from a couple of batches of Guy Arabs, this was the standard chassis for double-deckers until 1957. However, the first such chassis to be delivered in 1950 was one of Southdown's rare excursions into innovation for it was mounted with a double-deck coach body by Northern Counties, specifically for the Eastbourne to London service. Exhibited at the 1950 Commercial Motor Show, it originally seated 44 – 28 up and 16 downstairs – but it was found to

be too heavy and rolled alarmingly on corners, which passengers found more than a little disconcerting. In 1952 it was up-seated to 58, but this made little difference and later the same year it was re-seated to 50 for private hire work. It seems a little strange that it was so troublesome when Ribble ran a number of double-deck coaches on Leyland PD1 and PD2 chassis into the sixties. However, they were of lowbridge design which may have made them more stable when cornering.

There is little doubt that the full potential of the underfloor-

'In Which They Served'

Sussex is a beautiful county. Even today, with sprawling housing developments, there is still a surprising amount of unblemished countryside and unspoilt villages. Back in the fifties and sixties most of these villages were accessible by bus, many by double-decker, giving strength to the slogan 'See the countryside from the top of a bus'.

In a typical Southdown setting with the rolling Sussex Downs behind, all-Leyland PD2/1 322 (JCD 22) waits at Balcombe whilst *en route* for Horsham. *(P M Photography)*

By May 1969 when this photograph was taken most of the more rural services had been converted to one-man single-deck operation. The 32 from Brighton to Uckfield, however, had always been worked by single-deckers. Marshall-bodied Leyland Leopard 664 (264 AUF) passes through Fletching, unnoticed by the couple cleaning their Mini. *(Martin Llewellyn/Omnicolour)*

John C Beadle of Dartford had not built any double-deckers for several years, but in 1956 they bodied twelve Leyland PD2/12s for Southdown. They were built on Park Royal frames and consequently were virtually identical to the 'PUF'-registered Guys, although there were minor differences. 786 (RUF 186) is seen in September 1967 passing under Portsmouth & Southsea high level station. Following its withdrawal in 1971, the bus found its way to France but was repatriated and is now in preservation, beautifully restored. Just visible is the translucent roof panel, these being fitted to a handful of Southdown double-deckers. *(David Christie)*

Southdown's final Leyland PD2/12s were also the last half-cabs to be bought new and were probably 'la crème de la crème'. Twenty four in number they carried 59-seat bodies by East Lancashire Coachbuilders, and although very much to Southdown specification were basically the standard East Lancs product of the time (East Lancs was one of the few concerns still building bodies of five bay construction). The profile was more subtle than their Park Royal and Beadle counterparts, with more gentle curves and for some reason that is difficult to describe, they seemed somehow to represent traditional Southdown at its very best. Although not visible in this view, an interesting feature was the fitting of a sliding platform door, which slid forward, a hinged lower section ingeniously running behind the rear wheels. Car 808 (RUF 208) waits at the Tunbridge Wells terminus of jointly-operated service 119 from Brighton. *(John Kaye)*

In 1949 the Lioness was still being featured on the Coach Cruise brochure.

1950 Coach Tour advert. *(Author's Collection)*

The first of the new post-war touring coaches bought by Southdown was car 800 (LCD 200), which had Duple 'Ambassador' bodywork. Later renumbered 1800, when photographed at Sheffield Park Gardens in the early nineteen-sixties its touring days were over and it had received 41 standard coach seats for excursion and private hire work. *(Cliff Essex)*

engined single-decker was not appreciated at the time of its introduction. It was seen merely as a means of increasing seating capacity and it was only towards the end of the decade, when economies became necessary it was realised that, with the entrance ahead of the front wheels, the type was ideal for one-person operation. More and more services were converted to o.m.o., as it was known, and that eventually led to a revolution in the industry.

On coaches, of course, the entrance position was not of such importance and the main advantage *was* higher seating capacity. However, there were other benefits notably that the driver was no longer isolated in his own little cab, but shared the main saloon with his passengers; a distinct advantage on tours and excursions. Also, in these pre-Disability Discrimination Act days, the vehicles had a higher floor line, affording passengers an improved view by allowing them to see over walls and hedgerows.

By 1950 Southdown's coaching operations were pretty much back to normal, although continuing petrol rationing imposed some restrictions. Nevertheless that year saw the Company re-introducing Coach-Cruising holidays to the Continent. 1955 then saw the introduction of a 'second tier' programme of coach holidays. Named 'Beacon Tours' after the Crowborough company purchased by Southdown in 1949, they used 37-seat coaches and the tours were 'centred'; i.e. instead of staying in a different town each night, they were centred in one place with excursions operated each day. The use of higher capacity coaches enabled the prices of these tours to be reduced, thus attracting a wider clientele. These were the pre-motorway days when coaches were restricted to 30 mph when a tour to, say, North Wales would take two days, with an overnight stop in each direction. On the credit side, passengers saw the towns and villages through which they passed rather than endless miles of uninteresting motorway.

In original form, Duple Ambassador 800 was featured on the cover of the Southdown Tours Brochure for several years. *(Author's Collection)*

Sheer unadulterated luxury. The interior of one of the Harrington tourers; delivered in 1952/3, showing the twenty-six reclining armchairs laid out in 2+1 fashion to give maximum space and comfort. *(Alan Lambert)*

There followed a further twenty Royal Tigers with 41-seat Duple Ambassador bodies, intended primarily for express work. In their outward appearance they were similar to the previous Ambassadors, but lacked the glass cove panels. They started a new numbering series at 1600. Car 1604 (LUF 604) was photographed working a Gosport to London express service. *(S J Butler/Southdown Enthusiasts' Club)*

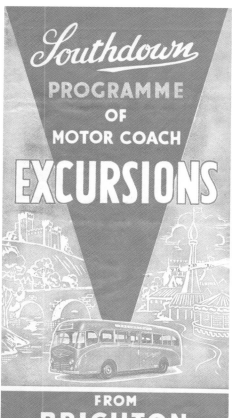

Left 1958 Excursion leaflet featuring an illustration of Ambassador 1603. *(Paul Gainsbury Collection)*.

Below A pair of fine Ambassadors! 1617 (LUF 617) of the second batch stands next to former touring coach 1808 (LCD 208) illustrating the differences between the two types. *(Cliff Essex)*

Following immediately after came another 25 Royal Tigers that were probably amongst the most 'un-Southdown-like' of all Southdown coaches. Their 41-seat centre-entrance bodies were built by Leyland itself to an angular design, virtually devoid of curves, that showed definite traces of transatlantic influence. Southdown managed to specify a straightened, very much stylised version of its frontal decorative beading but in all other respects they were the standard Leyland product. They were used primarily on express services and 1641 (LUF 641) is seen leaving Worthing Coach Station on a relief service to London. Ice cream, beach trays, blue sky and sunshine: everything about this picture proclaims 'Summer at the Seaside'. *(Southdown Enthusiasts' Club)*

These coaches were intended not only for express and excursion work, but also for use on the recently-introduced low-cost tours. One was featured on the cover of a brochure for an early 'Beacon' tour to Switzerland and the Italian Lakes. *(Author's Collection)*

In 1960/61 a number of these coaches were converted to dual-purpose status. 'Converted' was probably something of an over-statement for the 'conversion' consisted of fitting a bus-type destination box at the front. With a sliding centre door, they were hardly best-suited for stage carriage work but they were used regularly on the 30/32/36 group of services from Brighton and lasted in this form for around three years until their withdrawal. 1643 (LUF 643) waits to leave Pool Valley for East Grinstead. *(John Kaye)*

By the end of the decade Southdown coaches could be seen in most parts of Western Europe and between 1958 and 1960 even travelled as far as Moscow.

Express services were also expanding. The purchase of Triumph Coaches of Portsmouth in 1957 brought with it a number of express services, especially forces' leave services. A number of Southdown coaches were painted in Triumph's blue and cream livery to maintain goodwill. As a member of Associated Motorways and by joint working agreements with other operators, Southdown operated regular services to most parts of the country. Thus, particularly at weekends, one would see coaches from as far apart as Yorkshire, Birmingham and Devon edging their way into Brighton's already overcrowded Manchester Street coach station.

By 1957 Southdown had enjoyed its seven years of plenty but the end of the decade would see the beginning of a steady decline that would last much longer.

At the end of the Second World War, to help alleviate the acute vehicle shortage, John C Beadle of Dartford, long time supplier of bodywork to Southdown, hit on the idea of building integral buses and coaches using the running units from withdrawn pre-war vehicles. The coachbuilder had worked closely with Sentinel and other chassis manufacturers in producing this type of vehicle whereby, instead of a conventional chassis, the engine and running units were supported by a box-like body structure. By 1950 the idea had attracted the attention of several BET-Group operators, notably those in the South-East including Southdown, East Kent and Maidstone and District. In 1952 Southdown bought twenty of what became known as 'Beadle Rebuilds'. Originally 850-69 (LCD 850-69), they were renumbered to 1450-69 in 1959. They were 35-seaters, built to the maximum length of 30ft and were fitted with the engines and running units from pre-war 1400-class Leyland TS8s. Not surprisingly, they resembled the rebodied PS1s in appearance. However, the roar of the 8.6 litre Leyland oil engine soon dispelled any doubt as to which they were! 1466 (LCD 866) was photographed by the Riverside at Arundel in September 1962, appropriately working on route 66. (*Southdown Enthusiasts' Club*)

The final three of the Leyland Royal Tiger touring coaches were of interest in being Harrington 'Wayfarers' which were only 7ft 6ins wide. Delivered as 832-4 (OUF 832-4) they were almost at once renumbered 1832-4. 1832 was immediately transferred to the Ulster Transport Authority with 1833 following a year later. Both were used exclusively on Southdown tours of Northern Ireland until 1963. Their return to the mainland coincided with Southdown's takeover of Worthing-based Buck's Coaches and, to retain the company's goodwill, the two Royal Tigers were repainted into Buck's livery in which they remained until their withdrawal in 1966. Resplendent in Buck's cream and blue, 1833 waits for trade on Worthing sea front. (*Cliff Essex*)

Maintaining the sparkle! A further 75 similar vehicles were delivered during 1956-57 numbered 1040-1114 (RUF 40-74, SUF 875-914). There were some differences to the initial batch, notably the disappearance of the two small windows above the windscreen, a feature carried forward from the Duple design and, as it had with contemporary double-deckers, Southdown had at last relented and fitted sliding vents that, to suit the design, had square rather than the more usual radiused corners. All of the 1956 RUF-registered coaches were 41-seaters for excursion, private hire and express duties. Ensuring its appearance is maintained to the usual Southdown standard, 1054 passes through the bus washer in the yard adjoining Bognor garage, whilst sister coach 1066 awaits its turn. From the right the operation is being watched by London Transport Leyland RTL 383, which is enjoying an unaccustomed day by the seaside. (Southdown Enthusiasts' Club)

1102 (SUF 902) of the 1957 batch pulls into Victoria Coach Station with an express service from the Coast, showing off the nearside of the type.

Interior of a standard 41-seat Beadle-bodied Tiger Cub. *(Alan Lambert)*

Coach Tour Display Board *(G Kraemer-Johnson/ Ian Richardson Collection)*

PROGRAMME 1959

See Beautiful Britain

COACH CRUISING HOLIDAYS

by *Southdown*

Meanwhile Southdown's main coach cruise brochure for the same year continued to show the Royal Tiger. 'See Beautiful Britain' was Southdown's usual slogan for advertising its coach holidays. *(Paul Gainsbury Collection)*

SOUTHDOWN

We do the work... sit back and enjoy yourself!

BOOK NOW!

SOUTHDOWN

Continental

COACH TOURS

from LONDON and the SOUTH

Ask for full details from any Southdown office, your local agent or write to: Southdown Motor Services Ltd, Tours Department, Manchester Street, Brighton. BN2 1UF Telephone Brighton 66600 Telex: 87458

Best of the Breed

From 1956, with one or two exceptions, the annual British Coach Rally was held on Brighton's Madeira Drive. It attracted mainly independent operators; occasionally a coach would be entered by a B.E.T. or Tilling Group member, but they were few and far between. Southdown, probably because of its location, was a regular participant, sometimes entering two or three coaches and was a regular award winner as these pictures show. *(All are taken from the Southdown in-house magazine and are reproduced by kind permission of Stagecoach South)*

From MONDAY APRIL 13th
to SUNDAY MAY 10th, 1959

Southdown

· COACH ·
EXCURSIONS
· FROM ·
SHOREHAM

South Coast
EXPRESS SERVICE
Operated Jointly By

SOUTHDOWN MOTOR SERVICES LTD.
EAST KENT ROAD CAR COY. LTD.
ROYAL BLUE EXPRESS SERVICES
ASSOCIATED MOTORWAYS

DAILY SERVICES
LINK ALL THESE TOWNS
& INTERMEDIATE POINTS

From 26TH MAY to 19TH OCTOBER, 1963

MARGATE / BROADSTAIRS / RAMSGATE / SANDWICH / DEAL / WALMER / DOVER / CAPEL / FOLKESTONE / SANDGATE / HYTHE / DYMCHURCH / NEW ROMNEY / RYE / WINCHELSEA / HASTINGS / BEXHILL / PEVENSEY BAY / EASTBOURNE / SEAFORD / NEWHAVEN / PEACEHAVEN / BRIGHTON / HOVE / SHOREHAM / WORTHING / LITTLEHAMPTON / BOGNOR REGIS / CHICHESTER / EMSWORTH / HAVANT / PORTSMOUTH / HILSEA / FAREHAM / SOUTHAMPTON / LYNDHURST / BOURNEMOUTH

South Coast
EXPRESS SERVICE
Operated Jointly By

SOUTHDOWN MOTOR SERVICES LTD.
EAST KENT ROAD CAR COY. LTD.
ROYAL BLUE EXPRESS SERVICES
ASSOCIATED MOTORWAYS

DAILY SERVICES
LINK ALL THESE TOWNS
& INTERMEDIATE POINTS

From 21ST OCTOBER, 1962 to 25TH MAY, 1963
NO SERVICE CHRISTMAS DAY

MARGATE / BROADSTAIRS / RAMSGATE / SANDWICH / DEAL / WALMER / DOVER / CAPEL / FOLKESTONE / SANDGATE / HYTHE / DYMCHURCH / NEW ROMNEY / RYE / WINCHELSEA / HASTINGS / BEXHILL / PEVENSEY BAY / EASTBOURNE / SEAFORD / NEWHAVEN / PEACEHAVEN / BRIGHTON / HOVE / SHOREHAM / WORTHING / LITTLEHAMPTON / BOGNOR REGIS / CHICHESTER / EMSWORTH / HAVANT / PORTSMOUTH / HILSEA / FAREHAM / SOUTHAMPTON / LYNDHURST / BOURNEMOUTH

1959 Excursions from Shoreham with a Beadle-Commer on the cover. *(Author's Collection)*

The South Coast Express was normally the province of Leylands. Nevertheless, this 1962 timetable leaflet featured a Beadle-Commer. *(Howard Butler Collection)*

Over the winter of 1957/58 Southdown received 15 Tiger Cubs with Beadle bodies also to front entrance layout. The frontal treatment was a modified version of that on the integrals, but the Tiger Cubs retained their more curvaceous outline. Numbered 1115-29 (UCD 115-29), the seating capacities of the first thirteen were a mixture of 37 and 41 while the final two were 32-seat tourers. It was indeed a sad day when 1129 was delivered as it was the last Beadle body to be received by Southdown due to the closure of the Beadle factory. It was the end of a very long association between the two companies. Somewhat ironically 1129 was delivered in the blue and cream Linjebuss livery for which company it worked exclusively on that company's British tours until 1964 when it was up-seated to 41 and repainted in Southdown livery. 1126/7 were also blue and cream but with 'Triumph' fleetnames. 1127 is seen arriving at Victoria Coach Station. *(Alan Snatt)*

Interior of one of the front-entrance Tiger Cub tourers, 1128 or 1129. *(Alan Lambert)*

A new look – enter Mary and the Leopard

The tail-end of the 1950s saw a number of endings and beginnings within the Southdown empire. The last half-cab double-decker was delivered in 1957 and the very last Beadle body to be built for the company was received in 1958. The golden years of the early fifties was coming to an end. The increased popularity of television meant that people did not visit the theatres and cinemas so often; the introduction of the package holiday meant that many British families could afford to holiday abroad for the first time and, most significantly, private car ownership was rapidly increasing. All of these factors had an effect on the bus and coach industry. Passenger numbers began to fall and operators were forced to look for ways of economising.

Elimination of a conductor's wages produced a worthwhile saving and so came a steady increase in 'one-man operation' (o.m.o.) as it was known at the time. Early underfloor-engined single-deckers were converted to front entrance to enable 'pay-as-you-enter' operation and all new single-deckers were of this layout.

Pride of the fleet! The July 1958 issue of the Southdown Chronicle proudly portrays one of the first Northern Counties-bodied Leyland PD3s, in this case number 825. *(Southdown Chronicle/Stagecoach South)*

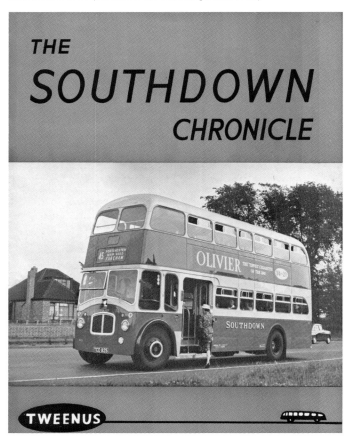

The maximum permitted length for double-deckers had been increased to 30ft on 1st July 1956 and to 36ft for single-deckers and coaches from 1961. As a result of these increases, Southdown abandoned its Leyland PD2 in favour of the 30ft PD3 to which it fitted a Northern Counties full-front body with a still modest seating capacity of 69 and, despite the variety of body-builders that had supplied Southdown in the past, this was to be the only type of double-decker to be purchased by the company for the next nine years: indeed until the front-engined chassis went out of production. The design changed over the years and it is interesting to see how it gradually metamorphasised into the panoramic version of 1967. No doubt because of its increased length these buses were given the nickname 'Queen Mary' quite early on. The name stuck and the type is now almost as iconic as the London Routemaster.

The second increase had more far-reaching effects for it meant that a single-decker could seat around 53, only slightly fewer than a Leyland PD2. As a result the single-decker began to replace double-deckers, firstly on rural routes and then on some quite busy interurban services on which they could be one man operated.

Whereas double-deck purchases had settled down to just one body and chassis type, with the coach fleet it was a case of 'all change' with two of Southdown's longest suppliers of coachwork disappearing from the scene. John C Beadle of Dartford ceased its coach building activities in 1959 to concentrate on its car sales business and 1966 saw the closure of the Harrington works in Hove. Southdown took coachwork by Burlingham, Weymann, Duple and Plaxton but by the end of the sixties, Plaxton was the only British coachbuilder still in existence and it became a case of 'Hobson's Choice'.

On the Personnel side, Arthur Woodgate died suddenly in 1961 following the death of his wife. His place as General Manager was taken by S J B Skyrme. 'Jim' Skyrme started his career in 1929 with the Belfast Omnibus Co. On qualifying he took up a position with the United Automobile Services Ltd, before moving to East Midlands Motor Services as Chief Engineer. He moved to the North Western Road Car Co. in a similar position before returning to East Midland as General Manager. Skyrme held the reins until 1966, when his place was taken by erstwhile Traffic Manager Gerald Duckworth. A Lancastrian by birth, Duckworth had joined the Company in the mid forties and had risen through the ranks to the top position. In 1972 he moved on to become Director of Manpower for the National Bus Company.

Co-ordination and company agreements continued to be made, a mileage agreement being reached with the London Transport Executive in 1958 to rationalise services in the rapidly expanding Crawley New Town. More significant was the agreement reached with Brighton Corporation and Brighton Hove & District which resulted in the formation of Brighton Area Transport Services (BATS), implemented in 1961, covered fully in the Photo Section of this chapter.

Several times in this book it has been noted that Southdown was not an innovative company, preferring the traditional and the tried and tested. However, in 1962 it caused quite a stir by breaking away in a completely new direction when it inaugurated the first Hovercraft service between Southsea and Ryde in the Isle of Wight. True, the operation lasted for only ten days but from 13th-22nd August 1962 what was termed an 'express service' was operated between the two points, using a Westland SRN2 Hovercraft that carried the Southdown fleetname (but not in Mackenzie script!).

A final event of some importance to occur in 1964 was the opening of 'Southdown House', a purpose-built office block built beside the entrance to the garage in Freshfield Road, Brighton. Head Office staff transferred to this building and the offices in Steine Street and Manchester Street were closed and eventually demolished.

Mr S J B Skyrmie, General Manager from 1961-1966. *(Southdown Chronicle/Stagecoach South)*

Mr Gerald Duckworth, General Manager from February 1966. *(Southdown Chronicle/Stagecoach South)*

1959 was a particularly hot summer and when the next twenty PD3s were delivered at the end of that year, they were fitted with opening front vents on the upper deck, which caused the disappearance of the traditional Northern Counties' radiused top corners, and to the nearside windscreen. As a result, the appearance of these buses was considerably altered, losing some of their sad expression although the lower edge of the windscreen still made them look rather unhappy. 861 (XUF 861) has just passed through another narrow bridge, this one in Tongdean Lane, Brighton. *(Southdown Enthusiasts' Club)*

See the Countryside by Bus – PD3
(Author's Collection)

Over the winter and spring of 1961/62, a further 40 Queen Marys arrived. Although outwardly similar, they were very different mechanically, being PD3/5s with semi-automatic pneumo-cyclic gearboxes. They were not a success. They could be easily identified by the clattering emanating from the clutch when the engine was idling and, in spite of modifications, they rolled back when making a hill start. After efforts to cure these problems had failed, they were transferred to West Sussex where they could work on flatter terrain. Other features included fluorescent lighting for the first time and illuminated offside advert panels, a popular innovation at the time. Number 917 (6917 CD) is seen working circular service 7 in Worthing, home for unloved buses. *(Keith Page/Southdown Enthusiasts' Club)*

In 1964/5, thirty Leyland PD3/4s were delivered with detachable tops for use on seasonal open-top services but which, with tops in place, could be used on normal services during the winter months. 422 (422 DCD), in summer guise, waits at the top of Beachy Head before returning to Eastbourne. *(Southdown Enthusiasts' Club)*

No doubt due to the poor performance of the pneumocyclic PD3s, the 1964 delivery saw a return to the PD3/4, 25 of which were received; 953-977 (953-977 CUF). They retained the offside illuminated advert panel but, apart from the chassis type, they differed in a number of ways from the previous batch. Most noticeable were the twin headlights and, at the rear, the destination display was reduced to a route-number only. The skirt panels were extended downward, obviating the need for lifeguard rails. The interior was improved by having wood-grain Formica on side panels and seat backs. 973 seen here in South Parade, Southsea when new, was one of two delivered with fixed glass in place of the usual ventilators in the front upper-deck windows, but they were quickly modified. Following the bus is a BMC removal lorry and behind that a stylish Riley saloon. And just look at the line up of British cars on the left! (Southdown Enthusiasts' Club)

Is it a plane? Is it a boat? No, it's a bus! For ten days in August 1962 staid, traditionalist Southdown made one of its rare flights of fancy; literally. In conjunction with Westland Hovercraft, it inaugurated a Hovercraft service between Southsea and Ryde in the Isle of Wight. Categorised as an 'Express Service', it was operated by a Westland SRN2 Hovercraft, which proudly carried the Southdown name above the windows. It seems that Southdown had high hopes of becoming hovercraft operators in a big way with plans for a Margate to Penzance service as well as cross-Channel operations. (Surfleet/ Southdown Enthusiasts' Club)

The 'Panoramics' as they became known, soon proved to be uncomfortably hot, particularly on the upper-deck. To reduce the problem, push-out vents, taken from the top decks of the convertibles, were fitted in their domes. This left the donors with an odd one-eyed appearance, but presumably the assumption was that they would only have their roofs in place in winter when ventilation was less important. With its additional ventilator in place, 351 turns out of Steyne Gardens in Worthing. The curved rear lower-deck window looked a little incongruous on these buses. *(Alan Snatt)*

The bright and functional interior of the Harrington Crusader. *(Alan Lambert)*

For the lower-price tours and some express work, Southdown remained faithful to the tried and tested Leyland Tiger Cub but with Beadle out of the field it chose, perhaps a little surprisingly, the Weymann Fanfare the design of which, particularly at the front end, quite closely resembled the Beadle Rochester. In all twenty-five were purchased, fifteen in 1960 (1130-1144: XUF 130-44) and a final ten in 1962 (1145-1154: 8145-54 CD) The final four were 41-seaters, the remainder being of 37-seat capacity for Beacon Tours. In apple green with cream window surrounds, a cream flash below the windscreen and dark green skirt, they looked particularly attractive and worthy additions to the fleet. They introduced yet another variety of opening ventilator in the form of 'Auster louvre-lights', similar to the Rotovent in directing air upwards, but neater in appearance and more effective in operation. They are clearly illustrated in this view of 1148 of the 1962 batch, seen arriving on Brighton's Marine Parade on what is obviously a glorious summer's day, with holidaymakers thronging the road and pavements behind. Unfortunately by this time it had, along with its fellows, lost its cream relief and adopted all-over green.
(Southdown Enthusiasts' Club)

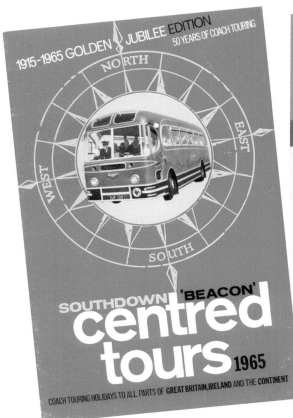

FINGER TIP CONTROL

for three-position adjustable passenger seats....
Big wide seats contoured to give you comfort and pleasure....
Streamlined for luxury and designed for the setting of your choice.

Printed in England by Graphic Art Services (Brighton) Limited

WINNER of Crew Award for SMARTEST Driver in the 11th. British Coach Rally 1965

SOUTHDOWN DRIVER - COURIER

Brochures featuring Weymann Fanfares

1965 Beacon Tours brochure featuring Weymann Fanfare. *(Paul Gainsbury Collection)*

1965 Golden Jubilee Tour Brochure – inside. *(The late Roger Knight Collection)*

By 1961, although immaculately maintained, the Royal Tiger tourers were becoming a little long in the tooth and so, between 1961 and 1963 no fewer than fifty-two new touring coaches were added to the fleet. They were based on the recently introduced Leyland Leopard L1 chassis powered by the O.600 engine as had been used in the Royal Tiger. Bodywork was supplied by Thomas Harrington to their Cavalier design, surely an all-time classic and one of the most elegant – dare I say – beautiful coaches of all time; certainly on underfloor-engined chassis. Southdown's examples were probably the ultimate, not only in looks but in appointment. They continued the tradition of 2+1 seating, having a capacity of just 28. Glass quarter lights were fitted together with a tubular steel parcels rack, on the offside only, ensuring that the passengers' upward view was obstructed as little as possible. Delivered with cream upper-works, 1725 (2725 CD) had lost them in favour of apple green when photographed in January 1964. *(Southdown Enthusiasts' Club)*

Southdown
PROGRAMME OF MOTOR COACH EXCURSIONS

FROM

EASTBOURNE

DURING

1957

SEATS MAY BE BOOKED AT

Southdown Coach Station 32 Cavendish Place *(main departure point)*	TELEPHONE **EASTBOURNE 3540**	Southdown Office 1 Cavendish Place *(opposite the Pier)*

Special Events and Race Meetings.—Excursions will be run to Race Meetings and other Special Events, including those shown below :—

	Time	Fare
GOODWOOD MOTOR RACES—22nd April, 10th June, 28th September	10 a.m.	11/9
BRANDS HATCH RACING—Car : 22nd April, 8th or 9th June, 5th August, 6th October, 26th December	9 a.m.	10/6
PORTSMOUTH (NAVY DAYS)—4th and 5th August ...	9 a.m.	11/9
EPSOM, DERBY WEEK ... ... *Derby Day* 5th June	8 a.m.	15/-
Other Days 4th, 6th, 7th June	10 a.m.	9/3
ROYAL ASCOT WEEK—18th, 19th, 20th, 21st June	8 a.m.	14/6
GOODWOOD WEEK—30th and 31st July, 1st and 2nd August	9 a.m.	11/9
FARNBOROUGH AIR SHOW—September 7th and 8th	9 a.m.	14/-
LEONARDSLEA GARDENS—Wednesdays, 8th, 15th, 22nd, 29th May ; Thursdays, 9th, 16th, 23rd, 30th May ; Saturdays, 4th, 11th, 18th, 25th May ; 1st June	2 p.m.	7/6
PENSHURST PLACE—when advertised	2 p.m.	9/-
CHARTWELL GARDENS—Wednesday, 19th June ...	2 p.m.	9/6

MORNING DRIVES, at 10.45 a.m., selected from :—

Herstmonceux Circular, 2/3 ; South Downs Circular, 2/3 ; Pevensey Castle, 1/9 ; Wannock Gardens, 1/9.

EVENING TRIPS, from 6 p.m.

Top Left 1957 leaflet 'Excursions from Eastbourne'

Top Right 1960 British Tours brochure showing Duple Ambassador.

Bottom Right 1959 BeaconTours Christmas brochure.

These two official photographs show the differences between the two batches of Weymann-bodied Leopards. *(Alan Lambert)*

Two of the 1962 Cavaliers had been based on the 36ft PSU3/3RT chassis, their bodies seating 49. In 1965 Southdown took delivery of a further 10 Leopards, built to 33ft length, with 41-seat Harrington Grenadier bodies, though retaining Cavalier fronts, intended for use on Beacon Tours (1754-63: BUF: BUF 154-63C). It was indeed a sad day when the last of these was delivered for it was to be the last Harrington body supplied to the Company, ending a very long and very close association between the two concerns. Harrington's coachworks ceased production the following year. This very nice picture of 1755 at Hastings, with the cliff railway towering behind, is a fine reminder of the elegance of Harrington's coachwork. *(Alan Snatt)*

The Quickest Coach Air Route to the Channel Islands VIA PORTSMOUTH AIRPORT

LONDON EASTBOURNE
KINGSTON BRIGHTON
GUILDFORD WORTHING
HINDHEAD LITTLEHAMPTON
PETERSFIELD BOGNOR REGIS
CHICHESTER
PORTSMOUTH
I.O.W

GUERNSEY

JERSEY

Southdown

CHANNEL AIRWAYS

SUMMER 1964

SPRING PERIOD

Southdown

EXPRESS COACH SERVICE

LONDON & BOGNOR REGIS

VIA MIDHURST-CHICHESTER AND VIA PETWORTH-LITTLEHAMPTON

SPRING PERIOD
From 10th APRIL until 1st JUNE, 1960

Decline and fall

The changes that had taken place during the early and mid 1960s were nothing compared with what was to follow. The British Electric Traction Company had been under increasing pressure to dispose of its bus operating interests and in November 1967 it capitulated and sold out to the Transport Holding Company (THC), the sale being completed in April 1968. The THC had been formed under the Transport Act of 1962 to take over the nationalised road transport operating and engineering companies formerly managed by the British Transport Commission (BTC), including the former Tilling Group companies and the manufacturing companies of Bristol Commercial Vehicles and Eastern Coachworks. It came into effect on 1st January 1963. With the acquisition of the BET group, most of the country's major bus operators were under one umbrella, ready for the creation of the National Bus Company.

The Transport Act of 1968, which came into effect on 1st January 1969, required the setting-up of Passenger Transport Authorities (later changed to Executives – PTEs), whereby all transport in the larger conurbations, whether state- or municipally-owned, would be co-ordinated and operated by the PTEs. Outside of these areas, the National Bus Company would be formed to take over those companies owned by the THC. This, of course, included Southdown.

Initially there was little outward sign of change. However, the NBC set about reorganising the constituent companies to create larger and allegedly more-efficiently managed companies. Thus, the small 150-vehicle fleet of Brighton Hove & District Omnibus Company Ltd, whose operating area was in the heart of Southdown territory, was absorbed by the larger operator.

BH&D's Bristols were totally non-standard to Southdown, but a number of Lodekkas were repainted in apple green and cream and had Southdown-BH&D fleetnames applied. Gradually similarly labelled Leyland PD3s were transferred to replace the older K-types, none of which ever received Southdown livery.

Vehicle policy, too, was changing. In 1965 Leyland Motors had taken a 25% share in both Bristol and Eastern Coachworks, which meant that these two companies, hitherto restricted to supplying only Tilling-Group companies, were now able to sell on the open market. Southdown's first Bristols arrived in 1968 in the form of Bristol RE saloons and the type became the standard single-deck chassis until the birth of the Leyland National. With the PD3 no longer in production, Southdown turned, perhaps surprisingly, not to the Atlantean but the Daimler Fleetline with Northern Counties bodywork well-up to Southdown's usual standard. However, the NBC had its own vehicle policy and the Bristol VRT with Eastern Coachworks body soon became the standard double-decker. The Leyland Leopard continued as the standard coach chassis with one final batch being bodied by Duple, the remainder by Plaxton.

BH&D buses became dispersed around the area with open-top Lodekkas serving Beachy Head and Hayling Island whilst objections from Southdown drivers dictated that most of the dual-door double-deckers ended up on former BH&D routes.

In 1972 the NBC introduced its corporate image. Subsidiary companies could choose between poppy red or leaf green with a white waistband the only relief (and that not always applied). Wheels were grey. A uniform fleetname style was introduced of white block letters with a double 'N' symbol in the form of an arrow. Southdown not unnaturally decided on leaf green, which was marginally better than the red that faded to a pinky-orange.

Also in 1972, the long-established London Coastal Coaches became National Travel (NBC) Ltd and the express services of all NBC's subsidiary companies were placed under the control of its Central Activities Group. Coaches were painted in an anonymous white with 'NATIONAL' in large alternate red and blue letters, while the company name was reduced to tiny red letters below the front windows; ideal for passengers trying to find a coach in Victoria Coach Station! Southdown's Coach Cruises were also passed to the Central Activities Group and the coaches similarly painted. When one remembered the beautiful dark green, apple green and cream of pre-war days….!

Southdown's final fifteen Daimler Fleetline double-deckers were delivered in July 1972. They had bodies by Eastern Coachworks, externally attractive but internally very Spartan compared to the Northern Counties examples. They were the last buses to be delivered in traditional apple green and primrose and, appropriately had Leyland engines.

The Southdown name was perpetuated throughout the NBC period and, of course, re-emerged as a private company following deregulation but it was not the same concern. The heart and soul had gone along with the Company's proud tradition – and it was certainly the end of 'Southdown Style'.